"God's amazing grace in Christ is 'the power of God unto salvation,' not only for the world but for the church and for life-long believers. Read this book and you'll be washed with 'wave upon wave' of the best news you'll ever hear."

Michael Horton, Professor of Theology, Westminster Seminary California; Co-Host, the *White Horse Inn*

"What is the Bible really all about? *On the Grace Of God* gets right to the point—grace, and more grace, for the undeserving. From cover to cover, this is the great message of the Bible, and Justin Holcomb proves it. If you are ready to believe the unbelievable, read this book. It will change you."

Ray Ortlund, Lead Pastor, Immanuel Church, Nashville

"*On the Grace of God* is a liberating study on something we can never get enough of—the startling and magnificent grace of God. In Jesus, John tells us, we have been given 'grace upon grace.' This book helps pour that grace upon grace on the heart of the reader, filling it with hope and joy in believing."

Sally Lloyd-Jones, author, *The Jesus Storybook Bible* and *Thoughts to Make Your Heart Sing*

"Amidst all the world religions and belief systems, *grace* is what makes Jesus followers different. There's nothing that can stop a heart that's been overwhelmed by grace. This book is a must read!"

Jefferson Bethke, author, *Jesus>Religion*

"The message of this book should never get old. Sinners saved by such astonishing grace will marvel for a lifetime that they've been rescued by such a God. More than that, we will marvel for all eternity at the personal manifestation of grace in the face of Christ Jesus. Go ahead now, sit yourself down with this book, get ready for heaven, and make yourself of more earthly good by meditating on the mind-stretching grace of God in which we are chosen, called, born again, justified, adopted, sanctified, glorified, and ushered into the very relationship with the God-man for which we were made. It is all of grace."

David Mathis, Executive Editor, desiringGod.org; elder, Bethlehem Baptist Church, Minneapolis

"This book offers a clear, concise, and compelling presentation of the grace of God. Many point grace out, and some might test it with their toes, but my friend Justin Holcomb is ever swimming in it, inviting all to join him. This will be now my go-to book recommendation on the subject."

Dustin Kensrue, Worship Director at Mars Hill Church;
Singer/Songwriter, Thrice

"Justin introduces great theologians to the reader in the same way he would introduce neighbors to one another at a backyard barbeque. Through relaxed conversation, Justin invites the authors of Scripture and great Christian thinkers to sit with the reader in the presence of the touchable and knowable God of grace. Simple but scholarly, *On the Grace of God* is that book you will want to put into the hands of everyone you know—those who do not yet trust Christ as Savior and those who do."

Judy Dabler, Reconciliation Specialist, Live at Peace Ministries;
author, *Peacemaking Women*

"*On the Grace of God* right-side-ups the upside-down-ness of our brokenness and broken thinking about God and his love. Since the Bible will not let us have virtuous ideas detached from their embodiment in Jesus—'God is love,' 'he himself is our peace,' 'I am the truth'—Justin Holcomb will not offer anything less than the glorious Jesus either. Brilliantly, honestly, and passionately, this book bleeds the gospel."

Jared C. Wilson, Pastor, Middletown Church, Middletown Springs, Vermont;
author, *Gospel Deeps*

"My friend Justin Holcomb wholeheartedly believes that the gospel of grace is *way* more drastic, *way* more offensive, *way* more liberating, *way* more shocking, and *way* more counterintuitive than any of us realize. He understands at the deepest level that there is nothing more radically unbalanced and drastically unsafe than grace. It is high time, in my opinion, for the church to embrace *sola gratia* (grace alone) anew. No more 'yes grace, but . . . ' No more fine print. No more conditions, qualifications, and footnotes. And, especially, no more silly cries for 'balance.' It is time to get drunk on grace. Two hundred–proof, defiant grace. Justin understands that grace is scandalous and scary, unnatural and undomesticated. But he also knows that it's the only thing that can set us free and light the church on fire."

Tullian Tchividjian, Pastor, Coral Ridge Presbyterian Church, Ft. Lauderdale, Florida; author, *Jesus + Nothing = Everything*

"*On the Grace of God* is just what we've needed: a scripturally rooted and deeply compassionate survey of how God's uncompromising love for sinners shines through the entire biblical narrative. How Justin Holcomb pulled off such a comprehensive feat in so few pages is a refreshing testament not only to his great learning and wisdom but also to his passion for reaching everyday men and women. Anyone looking to be encouraged by the unchanging and life-saving reality of God's grace in Jesus Christ should look no further."

David Zahl, Director and Editor, Mockingbird Ministries

"Holcomb brings great understanding of God's grace and love—a love undeserved and unconditionally given through the only one, Christ Jesus. *On the Grace of God* is an eye-opening, biblically rooted telling of the love story between God and his people. Where love and grace are many times misunderstood or misinterpreted, Holcomb sheds light on what God's true grace looks like."

Jake Luhrs, lead singer, August Burns Red

"Paul's stated mission was 'to testify to the gospel of the grace of God.' As twenty-first-century believers, that is our mission as well. But in order to do that, we must know God's grace ourselves. This book is a fresh reminder of how wonderful, matchless, and amazing is the grace of Jesus, a grace that is greater than all our sin. I was blessed in reading it and am sure you will be too."

Brian Brodersen, Associate Pastor, Calvary Chapel, Costa Mesa, California

Other Crossway books in the ABYAR series

On the New Testament, Mark Driscoll (2008)

On the Old Testament, Mark Driscoll (2008)

On Who Is God?, Mark Driscoll (2008)

On Church Leadership, Mark Driscoll (2008)

On the Grace of God

Justin S. Holcomb

WHEATON, ILLINOIS

On the Grace of God

Published by Crossway
1300 Crescent Street
Wheaton, Illinois 60187

Chapter 2 is adapted from "Sin, Violence and Sexual Assault," chapter 10 in *Rid of My Disgrace* (Crossway), copyright 2011 by Justin S. Holcomb and Lindsey A. Holcomb.

Chapter 3 is adapted from "Grace in the Old Testament," chapter 11 in *Rid of My Disgrace* (Crossway), copyright 2011 by Justin S. Holcomb and Lindsey A. Holcomb.

Chapter 4 is adapted from "Grace in the New Testament," chapter 12 in *Rid of My Disgrace* (Crossway), copyright 2011 by Justin S. Holcomb and Lindsey A. Holcomb.

Cover design: Patrick Mahoney of The Mahoney Design Team

First printing 2013

Printed in the United States of America

All emphases in Scripture quotations have been added by the author.

Trade paperback ISBN: 978-1-4335-3639-7
PDF ISBN: 978-1-4335-3640-3
Mobipocket ISBN: 978-1-4335-3641-0
ePub ISBN: 978-1-4335-3642-7

Library of Congress Cataloging-in-Publication Data

Holcomb, Justin S.
On the grace of God / Justin S. Holcomb.
p. cm.— (Re:Lit, a book you'll actually read)
Includes bibliographical references.
ISBN 978-1-4335-3639-7
1. Grace (Theology) I. Title.
BT761.3.H645 2013
234—dc23 2012040085

Crossway is a publishing ministry of Good News Publishers.

VP 22 21 20 19 18 17 16 15 14 13
15 14 13 12 11 10 9 8 7 6 5 4 3 2 1

Contents

Series Introduction

On the Grace of God is part of an ongoing series of books the average person can read in roughly one hour. The hope is that the big truths packed into these little books will make them different from the many other books that you would never pick up or would pick up only to put down quickly forever because they are simply too wordy and don't get to the point.

The series A Book You'll Actually Read is part of the literature ministry of Resurgence (theresurgence.com). Resurgence is a growing repository of free theological resources, such as audio and video downloads, and includes information about conferences and training programs we host. The elders of Mars Hill Church have generously agreed to fund Resurgence so that our culture can be filled with a resurgence of timeless Christian truth that is expressed and embodied in timely cultural ways.

The very center and core of the whole Bible is the doctrine of the grace of God—the grace of God which depends not one whit upon anything that is in man, but is absolutely undeserved, resistless and sovereign.

J. Gresham Machen

Chapter 1

Gratuitous and Undomesticated Grace

Grace changes everything.

The outrageousness of God's indiscriminating grace always gets people stirred up. That's because "real grace," writes Michael Spencer, "is simply inexplicable, inappropriate, out of the box, out of bounds, offensive, excessive, too much, given to the wrong people and all those things."[1]

"Grace" is the most important concept in the Bible, in Christianity, and in the world. It is most clearly expressed in the promise of God revealed in Scripture and embodied in Jesus Christ. The deepest message of the ministry of Jesus and of the entire Bible is the grace of God to sinners and sufferers.

About grace, Cathleen Falsani writes: "You can call it what you like, categorize it, vivisect it, qualify, quantify, or dismiss it, and none of it will make grace anything other than precisely what grace is: audacious, unwarranted, and unlimited."[2]

In English, the word *grace* has to do with charm, elegance, beauty, or attractiveness. The word *grace* as used in the Bible has very little to do with what is commonly understood by the English word. In fact, Scripture tells us that grace isn't a personal virtue at all; rather, it is undeserved favor lavished on an inferior by a superior. Grace is unmerited favor or a kindly disposition that leads to acts of kindness.

This is the grace God gives to us. J. Gresham Machen writes: "The very center and core of the whole Bible is the doctrine of the grace of God—the grace of God which depends not one whit upon anything that is in man, but is absolutely undeserved, resistless and sovereign. . . . Christian experience depends for its depth and for its power upon the way in which that blessed doctrine is cherished in the depths of the heart. The center of the Bible, and the center of Christianity, is found in the grace of God; and the necessary corollary of the grace of God is salvation through faith alone."[3]

Grace is the love of God shown to the unlovely; the peace of God given to the restless; the unmerited favor of God. Others have defined grace wonderfully:

> Grace is free sovereign favor to the ill-deserving.[4]
>
> Grace is love that cares and stoops and rescues.[5]
>
> [Grace] is God reaching downward to people who are in rebellion against Him.[6]
>
> Grace is unconditional love toward a person who does not deserve it.[7]

Grace is most needed and best understood in the midst of sin, suffering, and brokenness. We live in a world of earning, deserving, and merit. And these result in judgment. "Condemnation comes by merit; salvation comes only by grace: condemnation is earned by man; salvation is given by God."[8] That is why everyone wants and needs grace. Judgment kills. Only grace makes alive.[9]

The shorthand for grace is "mercy, not merit." Grace is getting what you don't deserve and *not* getting what you do deserve. Karma is all about getting what you deserve. Christianity teaches that getting what you deserve is death with no hope of resurrection. Grace is the opposite of karma. While everyone desperately needs it, grace is not about us. *Grace* is fundamentally a word about God: his uncoerced initiative and pervasive, extravagant demonstrations of care and favor.[10] Michael Horton writes: "In grace, God gives nothing less than Himself. Grace, then, is not a third thing or substance mediating between God and sinners, but is Jesus Christ in redeeming action."[11] Grace is as complete as God himself and expresses the quality of his own character. Karl Barth explains: "Grace is the very essence of the being of God. . . . God Himself is in it. He reveals His very essence in this streaming forth of grace."[12] God's action of grace is inexhaustible. That is why we find such superlative adjectives used by Paul to describe grace: "abundance of grace,"[a] "sufficient grace,"[b] "surpassing riches of grace."[c]

In the Christian tradition, there are many adjectives that have accompanied the word *grace*: amazing, free, scandalous, surprising, special, inexhaustible, incalculable, wondrous, mysterious, overflowing, abundant, irresistible, costly, extravagant, and more. My favorite is from John Calvin—gratuitous grace. *Gratuitous* is the idea of something being unwarranted or uncalled for. Though we yearn desperately for grace, the beautiful extravagance of God's love in Christ is utterly uncalled for. Gratuitous. In his *Institutes of the Christian Religion*, John Calvin writes: "We make the foundation of faith the

[a] Rom. 5:15, 17, 20; 2 Cor. 9:8; 1 Tim 1:14.
[b] 2 Cor. 12:9.
[c] 2 Cor. 9:14; Eph. 1:7; 2:7.

gratuitous promise, because in it faith properly consists. . . . Faith begins with the promise, rests in it, and ends in it."[13] In Calvin's theology, the knowledge of God the redeemer focuses on the "gratuitous promise" as the main theme of Scripture. The gratuitous promise in Christ is the substance of Scripture. The various terms denoting the gratuitous promise of God exist throughout Calvin's writings in countless variations: "gratuitous mercy,"[14] "gratuitous favor,"[15] "gratuitous goodness,"[16] "mere good pleasure,"[17] and "gratuitous love."[18] These expressions are also found throughout his commentaries, especially his *Commentary on Romans* and *Commentary on Genesis.*

God loves you with gratuitous grace, the only kind there is. God's grace is unconditioned and unconditional.[19] God is the one who loves in freedom. Unconditional love is a difficult concept to wrap your mind around. Many of us think (whether we admit it or not) there must be some breaking point where God gives up on us. Even if we successfully avoid believing this fallacy, others' overzealous cries still reach our ears: certainly there must be some sin or amount of sin that is just too much.

Because this is a common response to unconditional love, the human propensity is to establish negotiated settlements with God through religion. Robert Capon explains: "The world is by no means averse to religion. In fact, it is devoted to it with a passion. It will buy any recipe for salvation as long as that formula leaves the responsibility for cooking up salvation firmly in human hands. The world is drowning in religion. It is lying full fathom forty in the cults of spiritual growth, physical health, psychological self-improvement, and ethical probity—not to mention the religions of money, success, upward mobility, sin prevention, and cooking without animal fats. But it is scared out of its wits by any mention of the grace that takes the world home gratis."[20]

Religion tries to domesticate grace. But grace is antithetical to religion. T. F. Torrance explains the contrast: "Grace is costly to man because it lays the axe to the root of all his cherished possessions and achievements, not least in the realm of his religion, for it is in religion that man's self-justification may reach its supreme and most subtle form. . . . Religion can be the supreme form taken by human sin."[21]

Jacques Ellul likewise remarks, "Grace is the hardest thing for us to be reconciled to, because it implies the renouncing of our pretensions, our power, our pomp and circumstance. It is opposite of everything our 'religious' sentiments are looking for."[22] Grace reveals our natural pride of self-sufficiency, as well as the pride of spiritual progression. "Nothing is more devastating to spiritual pride than grace."[23] Therefore, our response to God's grace includes the recognition of our sinfulness and the rejection of all confidence in ourselves and our abilities.

Unmerited favor for undeserving sinners is never, ever comfortable. This is why religion tries to domesticate grace.

The grace from the gospel of Jesus Christ is the end of religion. Alexander Schmemann writes: "Christianity, however, is in a profound sense the end of all religion. . . . Religion is needed where there is a wall of separation between God and man. But Christ who is both God and man has broken down the wall between man and God. He is inaugurated a new life, not a new religion."[24] Robert Capon makes a similar point: "Christianity is not a religion; it is the proclamation of the end of religion. Religion is a human activity dedicated to the job of reconciling God to humanity and humanity to itself. The Gospel, however—the Good News of our Lord and Savior, Jesus Christ, is the astonishing announcement that God has done the whole work of reconciliation without a scrap of human assistance. It is the bizarre proclamation that religion is over—period."[25]

Grace is the end of religion because the secured promise of the gospel frees us from the supposed promises of our religious self-reliance, self-sufficiency, and self-justification. As we trace the biblical history of grace, remember that this same grace still has the explosive power to mess up all of your tidiest categories. The God of grace that shocked the world throughout Scripture has not stopped shocking the world with the radical grace of unmerited favor he lavishes upon unwilling rebels.

If this is all true about grace, then there are questions to answer. What does God tell us about his grace? Why does grace matter to us? Can this radical grace really be true? And what happens when this radical grace collides with sinners like us? This book will answer these questions as we explore the biblical trace of God's gratuitous and undomesticated grace, focusing on the grand narrative of God's grace in redemptive history.

What God Tells Us about His Grace

Three Words: Henna, Hesed, and Charis

God's overabundant grace is a major theme in the Bible. J. Gresham Machen writes: "The center of the Bible, and the center of Christianity, is found in the grace of God."[26] The entire Bible contains one big story, the story of the creation and redemption of the world by the God of grace. Scripture reveals that Almighty God is the God of grace. Over and over again he reveals his unmerited favor and kindly disposition through specific acts of unwarranted kindness.

What does the Bible say about grace? The biblical idea is conveyed through the Hebrew roots *henna* and *hesed* and the Greek word *charis*.[27]

The word *henna* is used over two hundred times in the Old Testament and is crucial to understanding the biblical concept of grace:

> [*Henna*] connotes favor, usually by a superior to an inferior, including but not limited to care for the poor, deliverance of those in distress, and other acts of compassion. Such beneficence is given freely, and thus can be requested, received and even withdrawn, but never claimed, coerced or possessed. The term often appears in the idiom, 'to find favor in someone's eyes', so that the prayer that [God] might 'make his face shine upon you' is tantamount to a request for him to extend his graciousness.[28]

What the word pictures is a petitioner approaching the throne of a king hoping to "find favor" in the king's eyes, thus receiving a favorable answer to his petition.

The word *hesed* appears even more than *henna* (over 240 times) in the Old Testament and refers to God's one-way love, mercy, and compassion toward his people. *Hesed* "refers to compassionate acts performed either spontaneously or in response to an appeal by one in dire straits."[29] These compassionate acts pertain to a covenantal relationship. God had made a covenant with his people. He promised to be a deliverer, protector, provider, and benefactor to his people. God's *hesed* refers to his unshakable faithfulness and dedication to these promises, which he has obligated himself to perform. This *hesed* is demonstrated out of affection and goodness: "God enters into covenant with human beings freely; the establishment of the covenant is itself an act of *hesed* on God's part. . . . *Hesed* includes notions of loyalty and constancy not always associated with *henna*."[30] As it states twenty-six times in Psalm 136, God's *hesed* lasts forever.

The Greek word for grace (*charis*) is used 156 times in the New Testament, and it's in every New Testament book. *Charis* is God's goodness, love, mercy, and kindness toward his people without regard to their deeds and in spite of what they deserve. It carries a connotation of favor, friendship, and kindness.[31] *Charis* is frequently used to refer to some form of heavenly favor shown to the human race.[d] Usually, however, when the New Testament speaks of heavenly grace, *charis* is explicitly defined as God's grace[32] or the grace of Jesus Christ.[33] About *charis*, Ralph Martin and Peter Davids write: "The entire NT and much early Christian writing is about the grace of God in Christ and its outworking in the believer. This is so whether or not the Greek word *charis* is employed in a particular passage."[34]

We learn much about grace from just these three words in the Bible:

> The vocabulary of "grace" connotes spontaneous kindness and acts of generosity grounded in dispositions of compassion toward those in need. "Grace" as a characteristic of God grounds divine-human relations in God's generous initiative and sustaining faithfulness culminating in the powerful, restorative activity of God on behalf of humanity. Of course, the concept of "grace" can be present, and often is, even when these and related words are absent.[35]

Old Testament

Exodus 34:6–7 is a great place to start in considering God's grace: "The Lord, the Lord, a God merciful and gracious, slow to anger, and abounding in steadfast love and faithfulness, keeping steadfast love for the thousandth generation, forgiving iniquity and transgression and sin, yet by no means clearing the guilty."[36]

God declares this about himself to his people, showing that grace is rooted in relationship and expresses the essence of God's character. Grace "outlasts his wrath and spills over in abundance in activity that saves and sustains life."[37] The fact that God describes himself as "abounding in steadfast love and faithfulness" right after his people have betrayed him and rebelled against him

[d] Acts 4:33; 6:8; 18:27; Heb. 13:9.

by worshiping an idol shows just how trustworthy and unfailing his love is.[e]

People can ask for God's favor,[f] but God sovereignly decides when and where he gives grace. He says, "I will be gracious to whom I will be gracious, and will show mercy on whom I will show mercy."[g] His choice to give grace does not hinge on a person's actions or how he responds—it depends purely on himself. This is how he can be gracious toward the unrighteous and sinners;[h] no one can "deserve" God's grace.

God's gracious character shines through in redemption, which is at the core of his identity: God describes himself as "the LORD your God, who brought you out of the land of Egypt, out of the house of slavery."[i] God has compassion, he takes the initiative to rescue his people from slavery, and he gives them a special place among the nations.

New Testament

In Matthew, Mark, and Luke, the extravagant grace of God is at work in and available through the ministry of Jesus. The seed of the word of God is sown without discrimination, regardless of the response.[j] In Matthew 8 and 9, Jesus is the presence, power, and grace of God's dominion to those marginalized in Jewish society: a leper, the slave of a Gentile army officer, an old woman, the demon-possessed, a paralytic, a collector of tolls, a young girl, and the blind.[38]

It is important to note that in Luke-Acts "grace" can be used as a parallel for "the gospel" or "salvation." Jesus's sermon at Nazareth

[e] Exodus 32. The episode of the golden calf.
[f] See especially the psalms, particularly Ps. 123:3; also see Isa. 30:19; Mal. 1:9.
[g] Ex. 33:19.
[h] Jon. 4:2, 11.
[i] Ex. 20:1.
[j] Mark 4:1–20.

is summarized as "words of grace,"[k] and believers can be said to have received "grace" or to be "full of grace" and be challenged to continue in "grace."[l] The missionaries in Acts proclaim the grace of God, and it is through this grace that people are able to respond with faith.[m]

Joel Green points out that Luke consistently grounds salvation in the ancient purpose of God, which comes to fruition at God's own initiative.[39] This reveals God to be the great benefactor who pours out his blessings on "all people."[n] Even the opportunity to repent is God's own gift.[o] The ministry of Jesus is the giving of God's salvific blessings to all who will receive them, and especially to those who are on the margins of society.[p]

John's Gospel strongly emphasizes God's love toward the blind, stubborn, and rebellious world. In John,

> the Son of God dwells in the love of the Father, and mediates that love to the world (see John 3:36; 5:20; 14:31; 15:9–10); he calls on his followers to love one another (15:17). From a different perspective, Revelation portrays the invincible love of God, sovereignly at work, spanning the period from creation to new creation, bringing his gracious purpose to consummation.[40]

Paul is responsible for nearly two-thirds of all New Testament references to *charis*. According to Paul, God initiates and is the source of salvation, and God's grace culminates in Jesus's work of redemption. Paul's emphasis is expressed in Ephesians 2:8–9: "For by grace you have been saved through faith, and this is not your own doing; it is the gift of God."

[k] Luke 4:22; cf. Acts 14:3; 20:32; see also 1 Pet. 5:12.
[l] Acts 6:8; 11:23; 13:43; cf. 20:24, 32.
[m] Acts 14:3, 26; 15:40; 18:27; 20:24, 32.
[n] Luke 3:6; Acts 2:17, 21.
[o] Acts 5:31; 11:18.
[p] Luke 4:18–19; 6:20–26.

Paul goes out of his way to make the point that God's grace is overflowing and abundant.[q] He also argues that grace motivates changed lives: "The love of Christ compels us!"[r]

Jesus Christ

While grace is expressed through the entire Old Testament and New Testament, Jesus is the deepest revelation of God's gracious nature: "an almighty power that at the same time is a boundless love so great it allows Him to be trampled upon and sacrificed to save the children He loves."[41] The ultimate expression of the grace of God is found in Jesus Christ: "grace and truth came through Jesus Christ."[s] Werner Elert writes, "Christ is not only the truth in person, but also grace in person."[42] Grace is what is meant in Romans 5:6: "While we were still sinners, Christ died for the ungodly." The very last verse of the Bible summarizes the message from Genesis to Revelation: "The grace of the Lord Jesus be with all."[t] Christ is the center of the Old Testament and the New Testament. All of this grace we read about culminates in the life, death, and resurrection of Jesus Christ.

We have seen that the message of Jesus, and the entire Bible, is the grace of God to sinners and sufferers. Jesus revealed the purpose of his ministry frequently:

> It is not the healthy who need a doctor but the sick. I came not to call the righteous but sinners.[u]

> The Son of Man came not to be served but to serve, and to give his life as a ransom for many.[v]

[q] Rom. 5:15, 17; 6:1; 2 Cor. 4:15; 8:9; 9:8, 14.
[r] 2 Cor. 5:14; cf. Rom 6:14; Titus 2:11–14.
[s] John 1:17.
[t] Rev. 22:21.
[u] Matt 9:12; Mark 2:17; Luke 5:31.
[v] Matt 20:28; Mark 10:45.

I have come to seek and save the lost.[w]

Capturing the texture of Jesus's ministry, Martin Luther writes: "Grace is given to heal the spiritually sick, not to decorate spiritual heroes."[43] John Calvin also summarizes this tone well: "In Christ, God's face shines out, full of grace and gentleness to poor, unworthy sinners."[44]

In a conversation with a Pharisee named Nicodemus Jesus revealed God's gracious disposition toward the world: "For God so loved the world that he gave his only Son, so that everyone who believes in him may not perish but may have eternal life. Indeed, God did not send the Son into the world to condemn the world, but in order that the world might be saved through him."[x]

Why Does Grace Matter to Us?

Grace is not an abstract principle but a reality of our life with God, as Karl Barth emphasized: "Grace must find expression in life, otherwise it is not grace."[45] And you can be assured that God's grace will embed itself into your life in profound ways. That is simply how the Holy Spirit works.

The grace of God extends down to us, not because we deserve it but precisely because we do not deserve it.[y] When we are born, we are dead, condemned, depraved, corrupt, perverse, sinful, and completely unable to save ourselves or even lift a finger to enable salvation.[z] Our works, even attempts at good works, are not adequate to contribute to our salvation. We are often tempted to believe it is the spiritual effort that matters.[46] But the intention of a dead man has no profound influence on a living God. Once the Spirit regener-

---

[w] Luke 19:10.
[x] John 3:16–17.
[y] Rom. 5:8.
[z] Romans 2–3; 6:23.

ates our dead hearts, we by faith receive the completed work of Jesus who accomplishes our justification—a declaration of his righteousness on us. As his grace continues to work in our lives, the gospel comes to fruition in every aspect of life.[aa] Through and motivated by God's grace, we are called to live in righteousness and holiness as God's adopted children, but we are not left to our own power. God has graciously sent the Holy Spirit to work in us to want to do and actually do true good works.[ab]

Our God of grace has a kindly disposition toward us, and throughout history he has demonstrated his grace in specific acts of kindness. He meets us in our places of hurt, sin, and brokenness and brings hope, healing, and comfort. It is in those seasons in our lives when the grace of God is most needed and best understood. The ultimate act of the God of grace is the ministry of Jesus: his incarnation, his sinless life, his death on the cross for the sins of the world, and his resurrection from the dead.

Our God of grace carries us all our lives, even when, and especially when, we are completely unable to move forward on our own. In fact, it is in our weakness that God's grace is made perfect.[ac] In our state of disgrace, he continually and always gives grace.

Disgrace is the opposite of grace. Grace is love that seeks you out even if you have nothing to give in return. Grace is being loved when you are or feel unlovable. Grace has the power to turn despair into hope. Grace listens, lifts up, cures, transforms, and heals.

Disgrace destroys, causes pain, deforms, and wounds. It alienates and isolates. Disgrace makes you feel worthless, rejected, unwanted, and repulsive, like a *persona non grata* (a "person without grace"). Disgrace silences and shuns.

[aa] Col. 1:6; 2 Pet. 1:3–9.
[ab] Phil. 2:13; Eph. 2:8–10.
[ac] 2 Cor. 12:9.

To your sense of disgrace, God restores, heals, and re-creates through grace. A good short definition of grace is "one-way love."[47] The contrast between disgrace and grace is staggering.

One-way love does not avoid you, but comes near, not because of personal merit but because of your need. It is the lasting transformation that takes place in human experience. One-way love is the change agent you need for the disgrace you are experiencing.

Can you receive grace and be rid of your disgrace? The gospel of Jesus Christ answers yes because "grace is embodied in Christ."[48]

Between the Bible's bookends of creation and restored creation is the unfolding story of God's redeeming grace. Biblical creation begins in harmony, unity, and peace (*shalom*),[49] but redemption was needed because, tragically, humanity rebelled, and the result was disgrace and destruction—the vandalism of *shalom*. But because God is faithful and compassionate, he restores his fallen creation and responds with grace and redemption. This good news is fully expressed in the life, death, and resurrection of Jesus, and its scope is as "far as the curse is found."[50]

Jesus is the redemptive work of God in our own history, in our own human flesh. James Fowler writes, "The historic incarnational manifestation of the redemptive mission of Jesus Christ is the basis for Christian grace. Grace was realized in Jesus Christ."[51] Scripturally, God's grace is so fully expressed in the person and work of Jesus that "apart from Christ there can be no talk of grace."[52] According to William Barclay, "Paul equates grace and Christ. Grace is Christ, and Christ is grace."[53] In the words of T. F. Torrance:

> Grace is . . . identical with Jesus Christ. Thus it would be just as wrong to speak of many graces as of many Christs, or of sacramental grace as of a sacramental Christ, or of created grace as of a created Christ. . . . Grace is the self-giving of Christ to us in which He both redeems and recreates us, such a self-giving

> that He invites us to Himself and makes us share . . . in the very Life and Love of God Himself.[54]

While God's grace is lavished abundantly ("to the ungrateful and the wicked"[ad]), his compassion reaches especially to those in desperate need. Martin Luther describes this good news: "God receives none but those who are forsaken, restores health to none but those who are sick, gives sight to none but the blind, and life to none but the dead. . . . He has mercy on none but the wretched and gives grace to none but those who are in disgrace."[55]

God's free grace invites our responses of faith, thankfulness, worship, and obedience. Describing the mystery and power of grace, Anne Lamott writes: "I do not at all understand the mystery of grace—only that it meets us where we are but does not leave us where it found us."[56]

Ultimately, God expresses his grace through redemption. To understand more about God's grace,[57] we will trace his redeeming grace through the Old and New Testaments. But before we do that, we will start with the bad news that because of sin we all need grace.

[ad] Luke 6:35.

Chapter 2

Why We Need Grace: Sin, Suffering, Evil, and Violence

In this chapter, we will investigate what the Bible says about sin, suffering, evil, and violence. Evil and sin work to infuse disgrace and violate peace.

In the Beginning

The Bible begins with God, the sovereign, good creator of all things: "In the beginning, God created the heavens and the earth."[a] God's creative handiwork, everything from light to land to living creatures, is called "good."[1] But humanity, being the very image of God, is the crown of God's good creation ("behold, it was very good"[b]). As the pinnacle of God's creation, human beings reveal God more wonderfully than any other creature—as they were created to be like God,[c] by God,[d] for God,[e] and to be with God.[f]

[a] Gen. 1:1.
[b] Gen. 1:31.
[c] Gen. 1:26.
[d] Gen. 1:27.
[e] Gen. 2:15.
[f] Gen. 2:15.

In Genesis 1:26, God says, "Let us make man in our image."[2] In the very beginning, our Creator gave us a remarkable title: he called us the image of God. This reveals the inherent dignity of all human beings.

To fully understand what "image of God" means, we need to look at the context of Old Testament history. Moses, the author of Genesis, and his Israelite readers understood these words because they lived in a world full of images. The most dominant images in the cultures of the ancient Near East were those of kings. Kings throughout the ancient world made images of themselves and placed them in various locations in their kingdoms. The pharaohs of Egypt, the emperors of Babylon, and the rulers of other empires used images of themselves as a way to display their authority and power. This custom of Moses's day helped him understand what was happening when God called Adam and Eve his image. Just as human kings had their images, the divine King ordained that the human race would be his royal image. Put simply, the expression "image of God" designated human beings as representatives of the supreme King of the universe.[3]

Immediately after making the man and woman, God granted them a special commission: "And God blessed them. And God said to them, 'Be fruitful and multiply and fill the earth and subdue it and have dominion over the fish of the sea and over the birds of the heavens and over every living thing that moves on the earth.'"[g] This verse contains five commands: "be fruitful," "multiply," "fill," "subdue," and "have dominion." These decrees reveal our most basic human responsibilities.

It was God's design that humanity should extend the reign of God throughout the world. This involves two basic responsibilities:

---

[g] Gen. 1:28.

multiplication and dominion. First, God gave Adam and Eve a commission to multiply: "Be fruitful . . . multiply . . . fill." Their job was to produce so many images of God that they would cover the earth. Second, God ordered them to have dominion over the earth: "subdue . . . have dominion." Adam and Eve were to exercise authority over creation, managing its vast resources on God's behalf. Having dominion means being good stewards of creation and creators of culture—not dominating.[4]

Richard Pratt argues that multiplication and dominion are deeply connected to our being the image of God. To explain this, he describes the ancient Near Eastern context:

> Many kingdoms in the ancient Near East stretched for hundreds of square miles. The kings of these empires were powerful leaders, but the sizes of their domains presented serious political problems. . . . Ancient kings simply could not have personal contact with all regions of their nations. They needed other ways to establish their authority. Many rulers solved this problem by erecting images of themselves at key sites throughout their kingdoms. They produced numerous statues of themselves and endowed their images with representative authority. . . . When citizens saw the images of their emperor, they understood to whom they owed their allegiance. They knew for certain who ruled the land.[5]

Moses described the twofold job of humanity against this historical background. To be sure, God had no problem filling the earth with his presence, but he chose to establish his authority on earth in ways that humans could understand. Similar to how ancient emperors filled their empires with images of themselves, God commanded his images to populate the landscape of his creation. In the command to "multiply," God wanted his images to spread to the ends of the earth. Just as an emperor conferred authority on his images, God commanded his likeness to reign over the world. His command to "have dominion" is God giving humans authority to represent him in his world.[6]

Shalom and Sin

In Genesis 1 and 2, we see that God's plan for humanity was for the earth to be filled with his image bearers, who were to glorify him through worship and obedience. This beautiful state of being, enjoying the cosmic bliss of God's intended blessing and his wise rule, is called *shalom*. One scholar writes, "In the Bible, *shalom* means universal flourishing, wholeness, and delight—a rich state of affairs in which natural needs are satisfied and natural gifts fruitfully employed, a state of affairs that inspires joyful wonder as its Creator and Savior opens doors and welcomes the creatures in whom he delights. *Shalom*, in other words, is the way things ought to be."[7]

Shalom means fullness of peace. It is the vision of a society without violence or fear: "I will give peace [*shalom*] in the land, and you shall lie down, and none shall make you afraid."[h] *Shalom* is a profound and comprehensive sort of well-being—abundant welfare—with its connotations of peace, justice, and the common good. While it is "intertwined with justice," says Nicholas Wolterstorff, it is more than justice. In *Until Justice and Peace Embrace*, Wolterstorff argues that *shalom* means harmonious and responsible relationships with God, other human beings, and nature. In short, biblical writers use the word *shalom* to describe the world of universal peace, safety, justice, order, and wholeness God intended.[8]

Genesis 3 records the terrible day when humanity fell into sin and *shalom* was violated. Adam and Eve violated their relationship

[h] Lev. 26:6.

with God by rebelling against his command. This was a moment of cosmic treason. Instead of trusting in God's wise and good word,[i] they trusted in the crafty and deceitful words of the Serpent.[j] In response, the Creator placed a curse on our parents that cast the whole human race into futility and death. The royal image of God fell into the severe ignobility we all experience.[9]

This tragic fall from grace into disgrace plunged humankind into a relational abyss. Paul Tripp writes:

> What seemed once unthinkably wrong and out of character for the world that God had made now became a daily experience. Words like falsehood, enemy, danger, sin, destruction, war, murder, sickness, fear, and hatred became regular parts of the fallen-world vocabulary. For the first time, the harmony between people was broken. Shame, fear, guilt, blame, greed, envy, conflict, and hurt made relationships a minefield they were never intended to be. People looked at other people as obstacles to getting what they wanted or as dangers to be avoided. Even families were unable to coexist in any kind of lasting and peaceful union. Violence became a common response to problems that had never before existed. Conflict existed in the human community as an experience more regular than peace. Marriage became a battle for control, and children's rebellion became a more natural response than willing submission. Things became more valuable than people, and they willingly competed with others in order to acquire more. The human community was more divided by love for self than united by love of neighbor. The words of people, meant to express truth and love, became weapons of anger and instruments of deceit. In an instant, the sweet music of human harmony had become the mournful dirge of human war.[10]

---

[i] Gen. 2:16–17.

[j] Gen. 3:1–5.

God's good creation is now cursed because of the entrance of sin.[11] The world is simply not the way it's supposed to be. The entrance of sin into God's good world leads to the shattering of *shalom*. Sin, in other words, is "culpable shalom-breaking."[12]

Evil is an intrusion upon *shalom*. The first intrusion was Satan's intrusion into God's garden, which led to Adam and Eve's tragic disobedience—the second intrusion. When sin is understood as an intrusion upon God's original plan for peace, it helps us see the biblical description of redemption as an intrusion of grace into disgrace or light into the darkness of sin or peace into disorder and violence. Just as sin and evil are an intrusion on original peace, so redemption is an intrusion into the fallen world, reclaiming what was originally intended for humans: peace.

Sin wrecks the order and goodness of God's world. Sin is the "vandalism of shalom."[13] Alvin Plantinga writes: "God hates sin not just because it violates his law but, more substantively, because it violates shalom, because it breaks the peace, because it interferes with the way things are supposed to be. God is for shalom and *therefore* against sin. In fact, we may safely describe evil as any spoiling of shalom, whether physically, morally, spiritually, or otherwise."[14]

Regarding this dimension of sin, Plantinga writes: "All sin has first and finally a Godward force. Let us say that a sin is any act—any thought, desire, emotion, word, or deed—or its particular absence, that displeases God and deserves blame. Let us add that the disposition to commit sins also displeases God and deserves blame, and let us therefore use the word sin to refer to such instances of both act and disposition. Sin is a culpable and personal affront to a personal God."[15]

God's image bearers were created to worship and obey him and to reflect his glory to his good creation. According to G. K. Beale, "God has made humans to reflect him, but if they do not commit themselves to him, they will not reflect him but something else in creation. At the core of our beings we are imaging creatures. It is not possible to be neutral on this issue: we either reflect the Creator or something in creation."[16] After the fall, humankind was enslaved to idolatry (hatred for God) and violence (hatred for each other). Sin inverts love for God, which in turn becomes idolatry, and inverts love for neighbor, which becomes exploitation of others. Instead of worshiping God, our inclination is to worship anything else but God. Idolatry is not the ceasing of worship. Rather, it is misdirected worship, and at the core of idolatry is self-worship.

Instead of loving one another as God originally intended, fallen humanity expresses hatred toward their neighbors. Sin perverts mutual love and harmony, resulting in domination and violence against others.[17] Both the vertical relationship with God and the horizontal relationship with God's image bearers are fractured by the fall. Evil is anti-creation, anti-life, and the force that seeks to oppose, deface, and destroy God, his good world, and his image bearers. Simply put, when someone defaces a human being—God's image bearer—ultimately an attack is being made against God himself.

The foundational premise of the Bible after Genesis 3, therefore, is that this fallen world, particularly fallen humanity, is violent.[18] The cosmic war begun by the Serpent in Eden, described in Genesis 3, produces collateral damage in the very next chapter. Immediately after the fall, there is a radical shift from *shalom* to violence, as the first murder takes place in Genesis 4. After God shows regard to Abel's worshipful offering, Cain responds by raging against God and murdering his brother.[k] The downward spiral of humankind and the constant spread of sin continues as God's blessing is replaced by God's curse.[19]

---

[k] Gen. 4:4–5, 8.

Violence is sin against both God and his image bearers. In our hatred for God, we hoard worship for self and strike against those who reflect God's glory. Cornelius Plantinga explains: "Godlessness is anti-shalom. Godlessness spoils the proper relation between human beings and their Maker and Savior. Sin offends God not only because it bereaves or assaults God directly, as in impiety or blasphemy, but also because it bereaves and assaults what God has made."[20]

A portion of the Old Testament is a catalog of cruelty. Widespread violence and the appalling evil of fallen humanity are recorded in detail on nearly every page of the Hebrew Bible:

> Acts of reprobate violence explode from the pages of the Old Testament as evil people perform unspeakable acts: Children are cannibalized (2 Kings 6:28–29; Ezek. 5:10; Lam. 2:20), boiled (Lam. 4:10), and dashed against a rock (Ps. 137:9). During the Babylonian invasion, Zedekiah is forced to watch his sons slaughtered, after which his own eyes are gouged out (Jer. 52:10–11). Pregnant women are ripped open (2 Kings 15:16; Amos 1:13). Other women are raped (Gen. 34:1–5; 1 Sam. 13:1–15; Ezek. 22:11); one of them is gang raped to the point of death (Judg. 19:22–30). Military atrocities are equally shocking. We read about stabbings (Judg. 3:12–20; 2 Sam. 2:23; 20:10) and beheadings (1 Sam. 17:54; 2 Sam. 4:7–9). These are normal military atrocities. More extraordinary cases involve torture and mutilation: limbs are cut off (Judg. 1:6–7), bodies hewed in pieces (1 Sam. 15:33), eyes gouged out (Judg. 16:21; 2 Kings 25:7), skulls punctured (Judg. 4:12–23; 5:26– 27) or crushed by a millstone pushed from a city wall (Judg. 9:53). Two hundred foreskins are collected (1 Sam. 18:27), seventy heads gathered (2 Kings 10:7–8), thirty men killed for their clothing (Judg. 14:19). Bodies are hanged (Josh. 8:29), mutilated and displayed as trophies (1 Sam. 31:9–10), trampled beyond

> recognition (2 Kings 9:30–37), destroyed by wild beasts (Josh. 13:8; 2 Kings 2:23–24), or flailed with briers (Judg. 8:16). Entire groups are massacred (1 Sam. 22:18–19; 1 Kings 16:8–14) or led into captivity strung together with hooks through their lips (Amos 4:2).[21]

The particular *shalom*-violating violence in the Old Testament is called *hamas*. In Genesis 6:11, 13, God decided to destroy the world in a flood because it was "filled with violence." Indeed, all violence is less than ideal when God desires perfection and peace, but often God must deal violently with *hamas*-violence. The great flood (Gen. 6:11, 13), punishment of the man of *hamas* in the law (Deut. 19:16–19), or judgment on the man of *hamas* in the Psalms (Ps. 11:5–6) are examples of God protecting his *shalom* from violent *hamas*.

Perhaps the most stunning of all violent passages in the Bible is the crucifixion of Jesus Christ. Isaiah 53:9–10 says:

> And they made his grave with the wicked
> and with a rich man in his death,
> although he had done no violence,
> and there was no deceit in his mouth.
> Yet it was the will of the LORD to crush him;
> he has put him to grief;
> when his soul makes an offering for guilt,
> he shall see his offspring; he shall prolong his days;
> the will of the LORD shall prosper in his hand.

Jesus was a man who had done no *hamas*, yet it was God's will to crush him. Indeed the cross was a violent death. But this was the climax of God's grace in restoring *shalom*. God offered up Jesus, who had done no *hamas*, as the sacrifice on behalf of all of violent (*hamas*) humanity to restore perfect *shalom*.

Hamas violence is a bitter fruit of the fall and is, without question, a "vandalism of *shalom*."[22] In biblical thinking, we can understand neither *shalom* nor sin apart from reference to God. David confesses to God, "Against you, you only, have I sinned and done what is evil in your sight, so that you may be justified in your words and blameless in your judgment."[l] Despite committing adultery with Bathsheba and orchestrating the murder of her husband, Uriah, David can write that he has sinned against God "only."[m] David's sins against other human beings were also, in the ultimate sense, transgressions committed against God himself. According to Plantinga, "*Shalom* is God's design for creation and redemption; sin is blamable human vandalism of these great realities and therefore an affront to their architect and builder."[23]

Evil and violence are not the final word. They are not capable of creating or defining reality. That is only God's prerogative. However, evil and violence can pervert, distort, and destroy. They are parasitic on the original good of God's creation. In this way evil serves as the backdrop on the stage where God's redemption shines with even greater brilliance and pronounced drama. What evil uses to destroy, God uses to expose, excise, and then heal.[24]

God's redemption imparts grace and brings peace. We turn to God's redeeming grace in the next two chapters.

---

[l] Ps. 51:4.

[m] See 2 Samuel 11.

Chapter 3

God's Redeeming Grace in the Old Testament

In the previous chapter, we saw the effects of the vandalism to *shalom* as generally expressed in violence. While the fall brought a curse upon creation, God did not leave his image bearers to rot under its effects forever without hope of rescue. Before the fall, Adam and Eve were "both naked and were not ashamed."[a] Post-fall, however, nudity became sheer vulnerability. More than polite embarrassment, shame implied the danger of physical exploitation and humiliation. We see this as Adam's shame soon festers into Noah's exploitation.[1] Nakedness and exploitation mark the earliest characters in Genesis and are traced throughout as a symbol of the depth of the effects of sin.

Originally, Adam and Eve were naked without shame, enjoying open harmony with each other and with God. Post-fall, however, they recognized that they were naked and ashamed—no longer holy and righteous. They were morally defiled because of sin.

---

[a] Gen. 2:25.

The Promise

From the very beginning, God made provisions through establishing sacrifices to deal with guilt from sin. After Adam and Eve disobeyed, they realized they were guilty and tried to cover themselves with fig leaves. God replaced their leaves with garments made from animal skins. This is the first demonstration of God's grace to fallen humanity. Where Adam and Eve's attempt at clothing themselves was rather poor (fig leaves would not last long), God demonstrated humility and grace by making by himself clothes for the man and the woman. The clothes he offered were much more durable and represented God's gracious willingness to continue providing for Adam and Eve despite their fallen state. Sinfulness had created a whole new group of needs for humanity, and God showed himself willing to address those needs *despite* sin.

Some Bible scholars propose that this is the first sacrifice in the Bible. A life had to be sacrificed before Adam and Eve were clothed.[2] E. J. Young, an Old Testament scholar, writes, "It would also appear that this act of God in the taking of animal life laid the foundation for animal sacrifice."[3] In this passage we see the pattern for all salvation history. God took a sacrificial animal (probably a lamb), slew it before the eyes of Adam and Eve, and wrapped the skins about their naked bodies. At that time, God gave them instructions about sacrifice and the covering of sins. The animal was God's gift. He furnished the skins to cover Adam and Eve. Since his first covering of guilt and shame, God has always provided his people with adequate covering for them to stand before him.[4]

God did not desert them to the futility of sin's harsh dominion. Even before covering them, God declared a plan to redeem them from sin and death: "And I will put enmity between you and the woman, and between your offspring and hers; he will crush your head, and you will strike his heel."[b] This declaration is about the hope for redemption, but notice the violence it involves—enmity, crushing, and striking.

Martin Luther called Genesis 3:15 the "proto-evangelion"—the first gospel announcement and promise concerning Jesus Christ. At first glance, a curse against God's enemy—the Serpent—may not seem like amazing grace. But this verse reveals God's plans to redeem humanity by his victory over Satan. The Serpent will continue to trouble Eve's descendants, constantly nipping at their heels, but one day the offspring of Eve will crush Satan's head in glorious victory. Even at the fall, God expressed his grace in word and deed, revealing that he is the God of grace.

This redemptive plan unfolded through the history of the Old Testament and was fulfilled in the cross and resurrection of Jesus Christ. The New Testament tells us that this wondrous destiny is ultimately realized in Christ, the greatest child of Eve. In his death, Christ destroyed Satan: "Since therefore the children share in flesh and blood, he himself likewise partook of the same things, that through death he might destroy the one who has the power of death, that is, the devil."[c]

When Christ rose from the dead he gained victory over death: "'Death is swallowed up in victory.' 'O death, where is your victory? O death, where is your sting?' The sting of death is sin, and the power of sin is the law. But thanks be to God, who gives us the victory through our Lord Jesus Christ."[d]

The final victory over Satan and the curse of death will occur when God's redeemed people inherit the new heavens and the new earth. As Paul told the Romans, "The God of peace will soon crush

---

[b] Gen. 3:15 NIV.
[c] Heb. 2:14.
[d] 1 Cor. 15:54b–57.

Satan under your feet."[e] Christ will lead his people to glory even as Adam led us into death.

Although Christ's ultimate victory over the grave is a future event, God in his grace has not deserted the human race to the horrors of futility and death. The testimony of Scripture is clear. Christ is the climax of a long historical process. God granted rich blessings in the exodus, in the Day of Atonement, and in the prophetic promises of the Messiah. He paved a way for his fallen image bearers to receive foretastes of the restoration and dignity Christ will give to his people.

The Bible attests again and again to God's persistence and desire for the redemption of his people: "God wants *shalom* and will pay any price to get it back. Human sin is stubborn, but not as stubborn as the grace of God and not half so persistent, not half so ready to suffer to win its way."[5]

God expresses grace to his people in his willingness to suffer for the sake of *shalom*: "Before the Fall the experience of wholeness flowed naturally from unhindered fellowship between Adam and Eve and between them and God. Afterward the experience of wholeness with God requires the grace of God . . . because of violence within and without."[6]

Separation from God and one another is a feature of the fallen order, whereas union with God and others is an essential feature of the gospel. Moving forward, we will explore the Bible for the unfolding themes of violence and redemption—or disgrace and grace.

Violence after the Promise

After the fall, the human capacity to injure others became consistently greater than the ability to show neighborly love. The raging

[e] Rom. 16:20.

cataract of violence that fills the pages of the primeval history in Genesis reaches a culmination in the flood narrative (Gen. 6:9–8:22): "The LORD saw that the wickedness of man was great in the earth, and that every intention of the thoughts of his heart was only evil continually."[f] Instead of the original "good" creation, we read that God's world was "corrupt in God's sight, and the earth was filled with violence."[g]

It was "violence" that intruded upon and violated God's creation (Gen. 6:11, 13) and pained his heart.[h] The "violence" and corruption (Gen. 6:11) refer to cruelty, oppression, and moral perversion. Stephen Dempster writes: "The world has become a frightful place under the rule of sin. The magnificent creation that once elicited the seven-fold 'it is good' has become a house of horrors. The creation is being raped by a humanity engaging in widespread evil."[7] In response to this, God determines to un-create his fallen creation through the judgment of the flood (Gen. 6:7, 17).

Redemption and the Flood

Even on this dark canvas of violence shine the bright colors of God's merciful redemption. God graciously spares Noah, who found grace and favor in his eyes (Gen. 6:8), but after the flood, we still read of the negative effects of sin. Even amid God's blessing of Noah we find the effects of the curse still remain.

Genesis 1–3	Genesis 9
God blesses humankind: "Be fruitful and multiply and fill the earth" (1:28)	God blesses Noah: "Be fruitful and multiply and fill the earth" (9:1)

[f] Gen. 6:5.
[g] Gen. 6:11.
[h] Gen. 6:6.

Genesis 1–3	Genesis 9
God plants a garden for man to enjoy (2:8)	Noah plants a vineyard / orchard (9:20)
Adam and Eve eat of the fruit and become naked (2:25; 3:7)	Noah eats the fruit of his vineyard and becomes naked (9:21)
Adam and Eve cover the shame of their nakedness (3:7, 21)	Shem and Japheth cover the shame of Noah's nakedness (9:23)
Curse (3:14–19)	Blessing and curse (9:25–27)

If the flood is an act of divine "de-creation" against human rebellion and sin, it is also an act of divine "re-creation" because of God's original good purpose. According to Paul Williamson,

> The climax of the flood narrative is best understood in terms of a "re-creation"—a restoration of the divine order and God's visible king-ship that had been established at creation. . . . The earth is made inhabitable by the separation of the land from the water (Gen. 8:1–3; cf. Gen. 1:9–10). Living creatures are brought out to repopulate the earth (Gen. 8:17–19; cf. Gen. 1:20–22, 24–25). Days and seasons are reestablished (Gen. 8:22; cf. Gen. 1:14–18). Humans are blessed by God (Gen. 9:1; cf. Gen. 1:28a), commanded to "Be fruitful and multiply, and fill the earth" (Gen. 9:1b, 7; cf. Gen. 1:28b), and given dominion over the animal kingdom (Gen. 9:2; cf. Gen. 1:28c). God provides humanity—made in his image (Gen. 9:6; cf. Gen. 1:26–27)—with food (Gen. 9:3; cf. Gen. 1:29–30).[8]

The message of the flood narrative is clear. Even in this fallen world, God can make all things new. Human depravity cannot stop God's steadfast love from blessing, saving, and restoring all those who trust in him. Despite the actions of sinful people, God's will is accomplished. His good purposes cannot be thwarted. This is seen clearly in the Genesis 9 narrative: immediately following the flood, God makes a covenant with Noah and his offspring (Gen. 9:8–11).

Noah, much like Abraham after him, represents a new beginning for humanity through God's gift of the covenant. Williamson writes: "The glue that binds all the biblical covenants together is God's creative purpose of universal blessing. Each of the subsequent covenants simply takes us one step closer towards the realization of that divine goal."[9] The redemption of God's people is rooted in God's covenantal faithfulness, his enduring steadfast love or *hesed. Hesed* is God's lovingkindness—"the consistent, ever-faithful, relentless, constantly pursuing, lavish, extravagant, unrestrained, one-way love of God."[10] It is often translated as "covenant love," "lovingkindness," "mercy," "steadfast love," "loyal love," "devotion," "commitment," or "reliability." In the Bible, God describes himself as having an overwhelming and abundant steadfast love and faithfulness toward his people. *Hesed* and grace describe God's goodness, love, mercy, and kindness toward his people without regard to their deeds and in spite of what they deserve.[11]

Hesed is the foundation for God's redemption and is seen throughout the entire Bible, especially in the Psalms.[i] The most repeated phrase used in praising God—"his steadfast love endures forever"—includes the idea of God's covenantal faithfulness, even if the word *hesed* is not present.[j] This means that the foundation of faith in God is God's enduring love for his people.

God's love moves him to compassion for his people. God's acts of redemption are motivated by his love and compassion. He feels his people's suffering.[k] God's love implies his jealousy for his

[i] Pss. 4:26; 92:1–2; 103:17–18; 106:44–45; 143:12.
[j] 1 Chron. 16:34; 2 Chron. 20:21; Pss. 92:12; 106:1; 107:1; 118:1; 136:1–26.
[k] Ps. 103:9–14; Isa. 14:1; 49:14–16; 54:7–8; 63:16; 66:16; Jer. 3:19; 30; 31; Hos. 11:8–9.

people as he pours out wrath on their sin and the sin that is done against them.

Redemption and the Exodus

Violence and redemption meet again in the exodus, the greatest divine act of salvation in the Old Testament. According to Dempster, "The story of the Exodus is the central salvation event in the Old Testament. The account of the liberation of a band of Hebrew slaves from horrific oppression in Egypt is the event that shaped virtually everything in the biblical imagination."[12]

The exodus brings three redemptive themes together: God compassionately responding to his people by freeing them from their bondage, atoning for sins in the Passover, and fighting against their enemy. These are all based on his promise to be their God and for them to be his people (Ex. 6:7; 25:8; 29:45–46).

The violence and redemption narratives in Exodus occur because of God's *hesed* for his people. This is clearly proclaimed in Exodus 34:6–7: "The Lord, the Lord, a God merciful and gracious, slow to anger, and abounding in steadfast love and faithfulness, keeping steadfast love for thousands, forgiving iniquity and transgression and sin, but who will by no means clear the guilty." It's precisely because of his *hesed* for his suffering people that God violently conquers their enemy.

Redemption and grace are central to understanding the themes of the exodus. Dempster writes: "Exodus language becomes the grammar used to express future salvation. Whether it is Hosea speaking of Israel going up from the land (Hos. 1:11), Isaiah of leading the people through the sea again (Isa. 11:15), Micah of Yahweh leading an exodus of crippled and outcasts (Mic. 4:6–7), Jeremiah of a new covenant (Jeremiah 31–34), the Exodus language of salvation is the way Israel construed its understanding of the future. . . .

Without this Exodus grammar it becomes virtually impossible to understand the language of the Bible."[13]

The narrative begins with God's people languishing in Egypt, enslaved to a murderous dictator,[l] and seemingly abandoned by their God. Yet God is "merciful and gracious, slow to anger, and abounding in steadfast love [*hesed*] and faithfulness."[m] And at their time of greatest need, God heard Israel's desperate cries for help. The covenant had not been forgotten: "Israel groaned because of their slavery and cried out for help. Their cry for rescue from slavery came up to God. And God heard their groaning, and God remembered his covenant with Abraham, with Isaac, and with Jacob."[n] In this passage, God shows more personal knowledge of his people, more compassion for those suffering, and more faithfulness to his promises to his people, than any one of them could muster for themselves. Redemption focuses on God's love (*hesed*) and not self-love.

The author of Exodus makes an explicit connection back to the God of the patriarchs. This means that God is a covenant-keeping God. He is the God of the patriarchs, "the God of Abraham, the God of Isaac, and the God of Jacob."[o] God "remembered" his covenant pledge to Israel, just as he had also graciously "remembered" Noah,[p] Abraham,[q] and Rachel,[r] in their times of greatest distress. This covenantal "remembrance" is intended to produce hope: "Israel's presence in Egypt is no product of chance. The Israelites in Egypt are to view their present suffering and oppression in light of God's larger, unchanging picture. God chose a people for himself and brought them down into Egypt. He will bring them out again."[14]

[l] Ex. 1:22.
[m] Ex. 34:6.
[n] Ex. 2:23–25.
[o] Ex. 4:5; cf. 3:16.
[p] Gen. 8:1.
[q] Gen. 19:29.
[r] Gen. 30:22.

In spite of major opposition from Pharaoh and "in the midst of the horrific genocide in Egypt, a child is born that is preserved from the holocaust. Moses is saved from the water and will eventually save his people from the water."[15] Moses, God's chosen deliverer, escapes death by being placed in an ark (same Hebrew word used for Noah's ark[s]) in the Nile River.[t] So the deliverance of Moses from the deadly waters not only looks back to God's redemption of Noah but also foreshadows a greater saving work yet to come in the Exodus narrative, when God saves his people at the Red Sea.

In the exodus, God is depicted as a divine warrior, completely sovereign and mighty to save. This story of God's people being delivered from the hands of their oppressors is filled with violence. This is a continued unfolding of the Genesis 3:15 promise. D. G. Reid writes:

> God's conquest of the Egyptian army in the Exodus event shapes an archetypal image of salvation in the Bible. It is a portrait of divine and redemptive violence in which God shows himself to be a divine warrior, superior to the powerful gods of Egypt (Exod. 15) and overthrowing the proud and mighty on behalf of the weak and the oppressed. Yet the Genesis story of Israel's descent into Egypt is fraught with violence within the patriarchal family (Gen. 37:12–36; cf. also Gen. 38; 49:5).[16]

However, this image of God's greatness and strength is not what the narrator focuses his attention on in the beginning of the story. The Lord, the God who keeps his covenant, is merciful and compassionate. In Israel's bleakest hour, amidst genocidal oppression, God mercifully remembers his covenant promises and draws near to his people.

---

[s] Gen. 6:14.

[t] Ex. 2:1–10 KJV.

> Not only does God hear, God also sees. And out of hearing and seeing, God knows the suffering of the people. These three words are repeated: first the narrator uses them in Exodus 2:24–25, and then God affirms them of himself in Exodus 3:7: "I have indeed seen the affliction of my people in Egypt. I have heard their outcry because of their slave-masters, and I know their sufferings."[17]

The Almighty sympathizes with the groans of his people. Another scholar writes, "God is not such a transcendent being as to be exalted above engagement with people. . . . God gets involved with their suffering."[18]

After remembering his gracious promises to Abraham, God responds by calling Moses to be the chosen deliverer of his covenant people.[u] God says to Moses:

> I have surely seen the affliction of my people who are in Egypt and have heard their cry because of their taskmasters. I know their sufferings, and I have come down to deliver them out of the hand of the Egyptians and to bring them up out of that land to a good and broad land, a land flowing with milk and honey. . . . And now, behold, the cry of the people of Israel has come to me, and I have also seen the oppression with which the Egyptians oppress them. Come, I will send you to Pharaoh that you may bring my people, the children of Israel, out of Egypt.[v]

God's rescue mission begins as Moses returns to Egypt and confronts Pharaoh. But instead of releasing the enslaved people of Israel, the king of Egypt increases their labor.[w] Yet, the cruelty of Pharaoh proves no match for the omnipotent mercies of the Creator, who commands Moses to declare to all of Israel:

---

[u] Ex. 3:1–4:31.
[v] Ex. 3:7–10.
[w] Ex. 5:1–18.

> I am the LORD, and I will bring you out from under the burdens of the Egyptians, and I will deliver you from slavery to them, and I will redeem you with an outstretched arm and with great acts of judgment. I will take you to be my people, and I will be your God, and you shall know that I am the LORD your God, who has brought you out from under the burdens of the Egyptians. I will bring you into the land that I swore to give to Abraham, to Isaac, and to Jacob. I will give it to you for a possession. I am the LORD.[x]

God then performs ten devastating plagues upon Egypt.[y] The culminating plague takes the life of every Egyptian firstborn son and persuades the hard-hearted Pharaoh to finally release his captives.[z] The purpose of these plagues was not to destroy but, rather, to display.[aa] God displays his righteous judgment against the hostile powers opposed to his people and his good purposes. He also demonstrates his magnificent saving power to all the earth.[ab] The plundering of Egypt,[ac] the parting of the Red Sea,[ad] and the destruction of Pharaoh's pursuing army[ae] inspire a song of praise for the triumphant God of Israel:[af] "Your right hand, O LORD, glorious in power, your right hand, O LORD, shatters the enemy."[ag] Out of sheer grace, God responded to the cries of his needy people and saved them to the uttermost.

According to Christopher Wright,

[x] Ex. 6:6–8.
[y] Ex. 7:1–12:36.
[z] Ex. 12:29–32.
[aa] See Ex. 9:16; Isa. 19:16–25.
[ab] Rom. 9:17.
[ac] Ex. 12:35–36.
[ad] Ex. 14:1–22.
[ae] Ex. 14:23–31.
[af] Ex. 15:1–21.
[ag] Ex. 15:6.

> In the exodus God responded to all the dimensions of Israel's need. God's momentous act of redemption did not merely rescue Israel from political, economic, and social oppression and then leave them to their own devices to worship whom they pleased. Nor did God merely offer them spiritual comfort of hope for some brighter future in a home beyond the sky while leaving their historical condition unchanged. No, the exodus effected real change in the people's real historical situation and at the same time called them into a real new relationship with the living God. This was God's total response to Israel's total need.[19]

Later biblical writers reflect upon the exodus as the paradigm of God's gracious salvation. Isaiah 43:1–3 reads as a poem of remembrance of God's redemption:

> Fear not, for I have redeemed you;
> I have called you by name, you are mine.
> When you pass through the waters, I will be with you;
> and through the rivers, they shall not overwhelm you;
> when you walk through fire you shall not be burned,
> and the flame shall not consume you.
> For I am the LORD your God,
> the Holy One of Israel, your Savior.

At the heart of the exodus lies God's costly and saving grace. And the pinnacle of this grace is the Passover.

Passover

Right before God delivered his people from their bitter bondage in Egypt through the exodus, he instituted a sacrifice—the Passover.[20] According to Dempster, "the Passover is the climax in a titanic battle that is waged between the God of Israel and the gods of Egypt."[21]

This battle reflects the original conflict between God and Satan in Genesis 3:15—the proto-evangelion.

According to God's instruction to Moses, every Israelite household was to select a year-old, unblemished, male lamb and slaughter it at twilight.[ah] Morris notes that the "animal was to be roasted whole and eaten that night, together with bitter herbs and bread made without yeast."[22] God tells Moses, "They shall take some of the blood and put it on the two doorposts and the lintel of the houses in which they eat it. . . . The blood shall be a sign for you, on the houses where you are. And when I see the blood, I will pass over you, and no plague will befall you to destroy you, when I strike the land of Egypt."[ai] Only those who are covered in the blood of the lamb would be saved. "The Passover lamb functioned as a penal substitute, dying in the place of the firstborn sons of the Israelites, in order that they might escape the wrath of God."[23] The shedding of blood averted divine punishment. Moses believed God's promise. He walked by faith. And he was spared. "By faith he [Moses] kept the Passover and sprinkled the blood, so that the Destroyer of the firstborn might not touch them."[aj]

In this one act of bloody sacrifice, through the slaying of a spotless lamb, God's people were protected from his wrath and consecrated to his holiness. The celebration of the Passover was to remain an annual reminder to Israel of the greatest act of redemption in their storied history. Successive generations were to remember what God had done in their midst: "And when your children say to you, 'What do you mean by this service?' you shall say, 'It is the sacrifice of the LORD's Passover, for he passed over the houses of the people of Israel in Egypt, when he struck the Egyptians but spared our houses.'"[ak]

[ah] Ex. 12:5, 6, 21.
[ai] Ex. 12:7, 13.
[aj] Heb. 11:28.
[ak] Ex. 12:26–27.

Dempster notes that this is the "second time in the larger storyline that a firstborn son is spared by the spilling of sacrificial blood (cf. Genesis 22). The narrative awaits a time when such a son will not be so fortunate, but whose spilled blood will save the world, not just a nation."[24]

Redemption and the Day of Atonement

God's presence with his people is a theme that can be traced in the Bible from cover to cover, all the way from Eden[al] to the new heaven and the new earth.[am] Not surprisingly, it is also a major theme in Exodus. During their wilderness wanderings, the Lord went ahead of Israel and guided the nation with a pillar of cloud by day and a pillar of fire by night.[an] God also manifested his holy presence on Sinai at the giving of the law.[ao]

Yet God's holy presence is problematic when sinful people draw near to him. Morris notes: "Approach to God was a tricky business in the days of Moses and Aaron. On the one hand it was the greatest of blessings and nobody wanted to be without God's promised presence. . . . But on the other hand God was awe-inspiring and powerful. To approach him in the wrong way might be disaster."[25]

How can a holy and righteous God dwell in the midst of a sinful and unclean people? The resolution to this problem comes in the book of Leviticus where we learn that the "relationship between a holy God and a sinful people can be maintained by sacrifice."[26] And the central sacrifice in the book of Leviticus is the Day of Atonement.

The Day of Atonement was the climax of the Old Testament sacrificial system and was a day of great bloodshed in which the grav-

[al] Genesis 2–3.
[am] Revelation 21.
[an] Ex. 13:21–22.
[ao] Exodus 19.

ity of humanity's sin could be seen visibly. Because of its importance, it eventually became referred to simply as "the Day."

The primary section in Scripture concerning the Day of Atonement appears in Leviticus 16–17. This passage functions as the center of the book of Leviticus, which itself is the center of the Pentateuch:

> [Leviticus 16] is like a hinge for the whole book of Leviticus. It brings to a climax all the preceding chapters about priestly duties in relation to sacrifice and to the diagnosis and treatment of uncleanness. The Day of Atonement provided an annual opportunity to "wipe the slate clean" by cleansing both the sanctuary and the people of all the defilements that had not been noticed and dealt with routinely. Fixed in the annual calendar exactly six months after the spring Passover, which celebrated the unique historical event of Israel's redemption, it provided the ongoing means of cleansing God's redeemed people so that he could continue to dwell among them.[27]

On this day, and on this day alone, the high priest would enter the Most Holy Place to atone for the sins of Israel in order to avert the holy wrath of God for the sins of the past year and to remove their sin and its stain from them. Two healthy goats without defect were chosen. They were therefore fit to represent sinless perfection.

The first goat was a propitiating sin offering. The high priest slaughtered this goat, which acted as a substitute for the sinners, who deserved a violently bloody death for their many sins. Atonement and blood sacrifice are wedded in the book of Leviticus: "For the life of the flesh is in the blood, and I have given it for you on the altar to make atonement for your souls, for it is the blood that makes atonement by the life."[ap] Commenting on this verse, David

---

[ap] Lev. 17:11.

Peterson writes: "Atonement here is not simply a matter of removing guilt or defilement by purging, but averting the wrath of God by offering the life of a substitute."[28] The substitutionary nature of the sacrifice is clear.

Then the high priest, acting as the representative and mediator between the sinful people and their holy God, would take the second goat and lay his hands on the animal while confessing the sins of the people. This goat, called the scapegoat, would then be sent away to die in the wilderness away from the sinners, symbolically expiating or removing the sins of the people by taking them away. "The goat shall bear all their iniquities on itself to a remote area, and he shall let the goat go free in the wilderness."[aq]

The scapegoat was sent away to a solitary place or a remote area, literally to "a land of cutting off." "Throughout Leviticus we find that to be excluded, or cut off, from the camp of Israel was to experience God's punishment for sin (e.g., Lev. 7:20–27; 17:4, 8–14; 18:29; 19:8; 20:3, 5–6, 17–18; 22:3; 23:29). The clear implication is that the goat is depicted in 12:22 as suffering this fate."[29]

Propitiation and Expiation

The slaughtered goat diverts the wrath of God from the people to the goat. This is called "propitiation." The scapegoat achieves purity and cleanliness for the people as it removes the guilt and shame of sin. This is expiation. The sacrifices of the Day were designed to pay for both sin's penalty and sin's presence in Israel. The shedding of blood and the sending off of the scapegoat were meant to appease God's wrath against sin and to cleanse the nation, the priesthood, and even the sanctuary itself from the taint of sin.[ar] This day speaks of the Lord's gracious concern both to deal fully with his people's sin

---

[aq] Lev. 16:22.

[ar] Lev. 16:30.

and to make them fully aware that they stand before him, accepted and covered irrespective of all iniquity, transgression, and sin.[as]

Propitiation is "an offering that turns away the wrath of God directed against sin."[30] Expiation removes sin and its effects because sin is "canceled out by being covered over."[31]

> Expiatory views of atonement focus on sacrifices as the way to free people of sin and its defilement. Propitiatory understandings of atonement present sacrifices as the appeasement of divine wrath. The symbolism of two goats on the Day of Atonement indicates that both concepts are essential in the OT imagery of atonement. The sacrificial system of the OT is presented as God's design for satisfying the just judgment of God but also for removing the guilt of sin from those for whom sacrifices are made.[32]

In both cases the ultimate goal of the atonement was to restore the relationship between the covenant God and his covenant people. "Sacrifice was the means of making the unholy pure again and restoring fellowship in the presence of a holy God who cannot tolerate the presence of sin and uncleanness. In other words, sacrifice was the means by which the central blessing of the covenant—communion between Yahweh and his people—was ensured and maintained."[33] The way of communion with God was through sacrifice. But the oft-repeated offerings for sin under the old covenant pointed to a greater sacrifice, a perfect sacrifice that was yet to come.

The Exile

After God delivered Israel from slavery in Egypt, he further demonstrated his grace in manifesting his presence among them in the

---

[as] Lev. 16:21.

pillar of cloud by day and the pillar of fire by night,[at] and in providing for their every need in their forty-year sojourn in the wilderness. After the death of Moses, Joshua lead Israel into the Promised Land, and God demonstrated his grace in delivering them from many enemies. After the death of Joshua, Israel repeatedly completed a cycle in which they rebelled against God and did what was right in their own eyes,[au] were oppressed by an enemy (such as the Philistines or Midianites), and called on God for help. God always demonstrated his grace by sending them a judge (such as Gideon and Samson) to deliver them from their enemies and establish peace again.

The last of these judges was Samuel, who anointed the first king of Israel, Saul,[av] and his successor, David, described as a man after God's own heart.[aw] After David's death he was succeeded by his son Solomon, who oversaw the building of the temple. Solomon's son Rehoboam succeeded him, and because he chose to be harsh with the Israelites, the northern tribes all seceded from the nation of Israel, leaving the northern kingdom of Israel and the southern kingdom of Judah. Throughout all these years there had been many times when, as a nation, both Israel and Judah rebelled against God. God demonstrated his grace by sending prophets (such as Isaiah, Jeremiah, and Elijah) to call his people to do one thing: repent—turn away from their sin and idolatry and turn back to him.

Ultimately neither Israel nor Judah repented, and in 722 BC the Assyrians conquered the northern kingdom of Israel, slaughtering thousands and thousands of Israelites and carrying the survivors into exile. The southern kingdom of Judah later suffered the same fate at the hand of the Babylonians in 586 BC. And yet prior to and even in the midst of these events God continued to demonstrate his

[at] Ex. 13:21–22.
[au] Judg. 17:6; 21:25.
[av] 1 Samuel 10.
[aw] 1 Sam. 13:14; 16:1–13.

grace by speaking words of comfort to Israel through the prophets. For example:

Prior to the exile:

> But now thus says the LORD,
> he who created you, O Jacob,
> he who formed you, O Israel:
> "Fear not, for I have redeemed you;
> I have called you by name, you are mine.
> When you pass through the waters, I will be with you;
> and through the rivers, they shall not overwhelm you;
> when you walk through fire you shall not be burned,
> and the flame shall not consume you.
> For I am the LORD your God,
> the Holy One of Israel, your Savior."[ax]

In the midst of the exile:

> For I know the plans I have for you, says the LORD, plans for your welfare and not for harm, to give you a future and a hope. Then you will call upon me and come and pray to me, and I will hear you. You will seek me and find me, when you seek me with all your heart. I will be found by you, declares the LORD, and I will restore your fortunes and gather you from all the nations and all the places where I have driven you, declares the LORD, and I will bring you back to the place from which I sent you into exile.[ay]

> Thus says the LORD God: Behold, I will open your graves and raise you from your graves, O my people. And I will bring you into the land of Israel. And you shall know that I am the LORD, when I open your graves, and raise you from your graves, O my people.[az]

[ax] Isa. 43:1–3a.
[ay] Jer. 29:11–14.
[az] Ezek. 37:12b–13.

So from the time of Joshua through the judges and the kings, all the way through the fall to Assyria and Babylon, God repeatedly demonstrated his grace, his *hesed*, to Israel.

Redemption and the Suffering Servant

The vision of an ultimate atoning sacrifice is literally personified in the prophetic vision of Isaiah 53. This passage paints a portrait of the suffering servant who is subjected to unjust violence for the sake of and in the place of others. Through substitutionary violence, the suffering servant brings *shalom* to sinners:

> He was wounded for our transgressions;
> he was crushed for our iniquities;
> upon him was the chastisement that brought us peace,
> and with his stripes we are healed.
> All we like sheep have gone astray;
> we have turned—every one—to his own way;
> and the LORD has laid on him
> the iniquity of us all.[ba]

The suffering servant becomes, himself, a sin offering so that sinners might be healed and forgiven. The suffering servant, the righteous one, through the anguish of his soul, bears the iniquities of his people in order that they might be counted righteous before God.

The "servant of the Lord" is described in Isaiah's four so-called servant songs.[bb] While the first three servant songs are often interpreted as referring collectively to the nation of Israel, the final song describes an individual. And not just any individual, but the Messiah.[34]

[ba] Isa. 53:5–6.

[bb] Isa. 42:1–4; 49:1–6; 50:4–9; 52:13–53:12.

In the fourth servant song, the identity of the servant is most certainly an individual who suffers in place of others. The servant endures violence on behalf of and for others. The sinless servant becomes a substitute for sinners:

> The Servant is explicitly said to suffer "for" others. The substitutionary character of his suffering is highlighted by the repeated contrast in Isaiah 53:4–6 between he, his, and him on the one hand, and we, us, we all, and us all on the other. The original Hebrew text underlines this even more forcefully by an emphatic use of personal pronouns. . . . A similar use of pronouns is found in verse 11, "their iniquities—he will bear them," and in verse 12, "for he—the sins of many, he bore them." All of this serves to underline the simple fact that the Servant, who is distinct from God's people, suffered in their place, as their substitute.[35]

Few passages in the Old Testament weave together more redemptive images and themes than this final servant song in Isaiah 52:13–53:12. Cole summarizes the saving work of the suffering servant:

> The servant sprinkles the nations, an idea with sacrificial overtones (Isa. 52:15). He takes on our infirmities and carries our sorrows (Isa. 53:4). He is pierced for our transgressions, crushed for our iniquities, and bears our punishment (Isa. 53:5). He substitutes for others. But in so doing he brings peace (*shalom*, Isa. 53:5). His wounds heal (Isa. 53:5). All this when we mistakenly thought it was God who was afflicting him for his iniquities (Isa. 53:6). He suffers for the sins of others, not his own. He is like a sacrificial lamb going to slaughter (Isa. 53:7). His conduct is exemplary (Isa. 53:7). Experiencing violence, he returns none (Isa. 53:9). He even intercedes for the transgressors (Isa. 53:12). He bears our iniquities and in fact bears the sins of many (Isa. 53:11–12). He becomes a guilt offering (Isa.

> 53:11). This is the offering that wipes out guilt (cf. Lev. 5:1–19; Num. 5:8; 1 Sam. 6:3–8). . . . His faithfulness leads to triumph (Isa. 53:10–12).[36]

The suffering of this servant is a violent affair. The servant "had done no violence," yet he substituted himself and bore in his own body chastisement that brings peace to others. Reid writes:

> Isaiah articulates a new and powerful vision of redemption in which violence is absorbed and transformed. In Isaiah 52–53 the heralding of Israel's divine warrior returning to bring Zion's deliverance (Isa. 52:7–12), suddenly gives way to a description of a suffering servant of Yahweh (Isa. 52:13–53:12). This representative servant figure, who has "done no violence" (Isa. 53:9), suffers violence on behalf of Israel, even to the extent of being "stricken by God, smitten by him, and afflicted" (Isa. 53:4). His triumph and exaltation (framing the passage in Isa. 52:13 and 53:12) is not a consequence of violent warfare but of his pouring out his life unto death (Isa. 53:12).[37]

The servant dies for the sins of the people and is "cut off out of the land of the living."[bc] Yet, he "shall see his offspring" and the Lord "shall prolong his days."[bd] This servant, "the righteous one," will justify and "make many to be accounted righteous."[be] In order to procure these blessings, the servant endures unspeakable evil. "From beginning to end, the passage emphasizes the appalling horror of what the Servant endured—far beyond what has ever been borne by any other human being."[38] He is a "man of sorrows, and acquainted with grief."[bf]

[bc] Isa. 53:8.
[bd] Isa. 53:10.
[be] Isa. 53:11.
[bf] Isa. 53:3.

Yet this servant not only has solidarity with humankind. The servant, while distinguished from the Lord in Isaiah 53, is also accorded divine status by the phrase "high and lifted up" in Isaiah 52:13: "Behold, my servant shall act wisely; he shall be *high and lifted up*, and shall be exalted." This Hebrew phrase appears only three other times in the Old Testament, all of them in Isaiah,[bg] and in each case they refer to the Lord. Alan Groves notes, thus "Yahweh's own lips declared that the servant was to be identified with Yahweh himself."[39]

So this passage is chiefly about the atoning work of a human/divine figure who will make "an offering for guilt."[bh] This phrase refers unmistakably to the guilt offerings described in Leviticus 5–7 as the atoning sacrifice for sins. "By using the same word here, Isaiah plainly intends to ascribe the same significance to the suffering Servant. Isaiah 53:10 thus anticipates something that will become explicit in the New Testament: the animal sacrifices of Leviticus are ultimately fulfilled in the sacrificial death of a person."[40]

Restoring *Shalom*

The Old Testament prophets are filled with images of a time when God would put things right again, and when *shalom* would be finally and permanently restored to God's creation.[bi] Plantinga writes:

> The prophets dreamed of a new age in which human crookedness would be straightened out, rough places made plain. The foolish would be made wise, and the wise, humble. They dreamed of a time when the deserts would flower, the mountains would run with wine, weeping would cease, and people could go to sleep without weapons on their laps. People would

[bg] Isa. 6:1; 33:10; 57:15.
[bh] Isa. 53:10.
[bi] Isa. 2:2–4; 11:1–9; 32:14–20; 42:1–12; 60; 65:17–25; Joel 2:24–29; 3:17–18.

> work in peace and work to fruitful effect. Lambs could lie down with lions. All nature would be fruitful, benign, and filled with wonder upon wonder; all humans would be knit together in brotherhood and sisterhood; and all nature and all humans would look to God, walk with God, lean toward God, and delight in God. Shouts of joy and recognition would well up from valleys and seas, from women in streets and from men on ships. The webbing together of God, humans, and all creation in justice, fulfillment, and delight is what the Hebrew prophets call *shalom*.[41]

The restoration of *shalom* is frequently united to the coming of the Messiah, the long-awaited deliverer, prophesied throughout the Old Testament. The hope of *shalom* was the hope of Israel. And the hope of Israel was the only hope for the world. According to the book of Isaiah, the hope of Israel was clearly embodied in the messianic child of Isaiah 9 and the suffering servant of Isaiah 53. This figure, the messianic child and the suffering servant of Isaiah, is one and the same: a suffering Messiah who brings *shalom*.

> For to us a child is born,
> to us a son is given;
> and the government shall be upon his shoulder,
> and his name shall be called
> Wonderful Counselor, Mighty God,
> Everlasting Father, Prince of Peace [*shalom*].
> Of the increase of his government and of peace [*shalom*]
> there will be no end,
> on the throne of David and over his kingdom,
> to establish it and to uphold it with justice and with righteousness
> from this time forth and forevermore.
> The zeal of the LORD of hosts will do this.[42]

Note, again, Isaiah 53:5: "But he was wounded for our transgressions; he was crushed for our iniquities; upon him was the chastisement that brought us peace [*shalom*], and with his stripes we are healed."

The New Testament writers clearly understand this suffering servant, this bringer of peace, to be Jesus of Nazareth. Isaiah 53 is directly quoted seven times in the New Testament as referring to Jesus Christ,[bj] and alluded to over thirty-four times.[43] In his perfectly sinless life and his substitutionary atoning death, Jesus secured salvation for sinners and brought them *shalom* with God.

Jesus Christ came into this violent world that was shattered by sin, and he suffered a violent death at the hands of violent men in order to save rebellious sinners, rescuing them from divine wrath, and supplying them with divine peace, mercy, grace, and love. The sinless one suffered disgrace in order to bring sinners grace. The light of heaven entered into the darkness of this world. "The people dwelling in darkness have seen a great light, and for those dwelling in the region and shadow of death, on them a light has dawned."[bk]

In our survey of the Old Testament, we have seen that the Scriptures do not avoid the issue of violence. "The Bible is not a 'nice' book that hides the sordid side of life. The Bible is a book of thoroughgoing realism. The Bible's stories of violence demonstrate the depths of depravity to which the human race descends. Paradoxically, though, the nadir of depravity represented by biblical stories of violence is also the climax of the Bible's story of redemption. The violence of the cross is the pivot point of redemption."[44]

And it is the cross of Jesus Christ, the pivot point of redemption, to which we now turn our attention.

[bj] Matt. 8:16–17; Luke 22:37; John 12:38; Acts 8:32–35; Rom. 10:16; 1 Pet. 2:22; 1 Pet. 2:24.
[bk] Matt. 4:16; cf. Isa. 9:2.

Chapter 4

God's Redeeming Grace in the New Testament

We have already focused on the radical shift from peace and *shalom* to violence and sin. We have seen that God's desire to restore peace and bring redemption is expressed throughout the entire Old Testament by tracing the themes of violence (disgrace) and redemption (grace). Now we will see how they converge on the cross of Jesus Christ:

> An entire episode of human history is sealed with the narrator's judgment that "the earth was filled with violence" (Gen. 6:11). The biblical logic of redemption, viewed through the canonical lens of the incarnation and the cross, allows no other course for its plot line than to run the gauntlet of human violence. But the outcome is a divine and dramatic resolution of violence, and the world-transforming power of the gospel.[1]

The Stroke of Grace

The cross is God's attack on sin and violence; it is salvation from sin and its effects. The cross really is a *coup de grace*, meaning "stroke of grace," which refers to the deathblow delivered to the misery of our suffering:

> Jesus' submission to the violence of the cross demonstrates God's will to absorb in the Son the wrath that is due to Israel and the world. Jesus' prayer to the Father from the cross, "forgive them, for they do not know what they are doing" (Luke 23:34; cf. Acts 7:60 NIV), memorably expresses the commandment to love one's enemies even as they perpetrate their violence. The cross embodies Jesus' victory over violence and is the climax of the biblical story of violence.[2]

In the cross God is not revealed in the power and glory, which natural reason can recognize as divine, but in the very opposite of divinity, in human disgrace, poverty, suffering, and death, in what seems to be weakness and foolishness.

God's desire for *shalom* and his response to violence culminates in the person and work of Jesus Christ. The life, death, and resurrection of Jesus fulfills redemption themes from the Old Testament: the Passover sacrifice in Exodus, God in Exodus as the divine warrior protecting his people by conquering their enemy, the sacrifices of propitiation and expiation in Leviticus 16, and the suffering servant whose suffering brings peace. This good news of the Bible is that in Jesus Christ, the God-man, our creator has become our redeemer.

This astounding reality is the best part of the good news. For this reason, the gospel of Jesus Christ occupies the central place in the New Testament as the message of first importance.[3] The heart of this message concerns the person and the work of Jesus Christ, that is, who Jesus is and what he has accomplished by his life, death, and resurrection.[4]

Tim Keller explains the scope and goal of the good news:

> The "gospel" is the good news that through Christ the power of God's kingdom has entered history to renew the whole world. When we believe and rely on Jesus' work and record (rather than ours) for our relationship to God, that kingdom power comes upon us and begins to work through us.[5]

Elsewhere Keller writes, "Through the person and work of Jesus Christ, God fully accomplishes salvation for us, rescuing us from judgment for sin into fellowship with him, and then restores the creation in which we can enjoy our new life together with him forever."[6]

To better understand that Jesus is the fullness of God's plan to redeem humanity, restore *shalom*, and replace disgrace with grace, we will look at who Jesus is and what he has done.

Who Jesus Is—God with Us

Augustine says, "There no hope at all except perhaps for the grace of the Incarnation."[7] This is a powerful claim. How is grace tied to the incarnation?

Like Genesis, the Gospel of John begins in the beginning.[a] John 1:1–3 tells us: "In the beginning was the Word, and the Word was with God, and the Word was God. He was in the beginning with God. All things were made through him, and without him was not any thing made that was made." From the very outset of his Gospel, John shines the spotlight on the Son of God, Jesus Christ. Christ is the eternal Word of God,[b] who was eternally with God,[c] and who was the agent through whom all things were created by God.[d]

The highlight of John's prologue comes in 1:14 when he writes: "And the Word became flesh and dwelt among us, and we have seen

[a] Gen. 1:1; John 1:1.
[b] John 1:1.
[c] John 1:2.
[d] John 1:3.

his glory, glory as of the only Son from the Father, full of grace and truth." According to John, the eternal, divine Son of God, the one who made all things, became flesh. In Jesus, God became a man and lived on the earth that he created. God took on flesh, which is the meaning of *incarnation*. In Jesus, "the whole fullness of deity dwells bodily."[e] In Jesus Christ, the invisible God has become visible: "No one has ever seen God; the only God, who is at the Father's side, he has made him known."[f] Therefore, God the Son makes known God the Father.

John goes on to say that our creator has become our redeemer. The Son of God came in the flesh in order to make possible the salvation of sinners: "He came to his own, and his own people did not receive him. But to all who did receive him, who believed in his name, he gave the right to become children of God, who were born, not of blood nor of the will of the flesh nor of the will of man, but of God."[g]

The divine Son of God has come into the very world he created on a rescue mission to save sinners from the wrath of God, condemnation, sin, and sin's effects. The rescue mission of Jesus is a key theme in each Gospel account but particularly in the Gospel of John.[8] This rescue is described as light intruding into the darkness: "The light shines in the darkness, and the darkness has not overcome it."[h] Jesus Christ, who called himself "the light of the world,"[9] entered into the darkness of this world to bring light and eternal life to sinners who are dwelling in the darkness of their rebellion and sin: "The people dwelling in darkness have seen a great light, and for those dwelling in the region and shadow of death, on them a light has dawned."[i]

[e] Col. 2:9.
[f] John 1:18.
[g] John 1:11–13.
[h] John 1:5.
[i] Matt. 4:16; see also Isa. 9:2.

Between his two claims to be the light of the world,[j] Jesus heals a blind man. The miracle of giving sight to the man born blind demonstrates the purpose of Jesus's ministry. It illustrates Jesus's power to bring his light to those in darkness. Where darkness, death, and decay had reigned, Jesus breaks in with light, liberation, and love.

A picture of this comes from Robert Louis Stevenson, the author of *Treasure Island*, who lived in Scotland in the nineteenth century. As a boy, his family lived on a hillside overlooking a small town. Robert was intrigued by the work of the old lamplighters who went about with a ladder and a torch, lighting the streetlights for the night. One evening, as Robert stood watching with fascination, his nurse asked him, "Robert, what in the world are you looking at out there?" With great excitement he exclaimed: "Look at that man! He's punching holes in the darkness!"[10]

The light of the world has entered into the world's darkness in order to punch holes in it and bring those who dwell in darkness into the dawn of his grace and truth. None of this would be possible apart from Christ's incarnation. But, in addition to rescuing us, the incarnation also means that God is present with us: "[God] comes for you, in the flesh, in Christ, into suffering, on your behalf. He does not offer advice and perspective from afar; he steps into your significant suffering. He will see you through, and work with you the whole way. He will carry you even *in extremis.*"[11]

The Gospel of Matthew introduces Jesus as the long-awaited deliverer of God's people. In the narrative of Jesus's birth, Matthew quotes Isaiah 7:14, an Old Testament prophecy about the coming Messiah who would save his people from their sins: "All this took place to fulfill what the Lord had spoken by the prophet: 'Behold, the virgin shall conceive and bear a son, and they shall call his name

[j] John 8:12; 9:5.

Immanuel.'"[k] Matthew tells us that Immanuel is a Hebrew name that is translated "God with us." Even though "Immanuel" is used only two times in the Bible,[l] we have seen that the idea of God's dwelling with humankind, his gracious presence with his people, spans the entire story of redemption. *Hesed*, God's covenantal love, is a repeated theme throughout both Testaments: "I will live among them and walk among them, and I will be their God and they will be my people."[m] So the hope of a Savior is found in this person called "Immanuel." And that person is Jesus.

While the Gospel of Matthew begins by saying that Jesus is "God with us," the rest of the book details what Jesus did while he was on earth.[12] At the end of Matthew, Jesus issues a glorious promise: "Behold, I am with you always, to the end of the age."[n] Matthew's Gospel begins with the prophecy that the Savior would be "Immanuel, that is, 'God with us,'" and it ends with Jesus's promise to his disciples: "I am with you always." In other words, the Gospel of Matthew tells us that the way God will be with his people is through a relationship with his Son, Jesus Christ.

What Jesus Has Done

Our knowledge of the life and ministry of Jesus Christ comes almost entirely from the four New Testament Gospels. These books detail what Jesus taught and what Jesus did during his three-and-a-half-year ministry in and around Jerusalem.[13] However, the central emphasis of these books is the atoning death and triumphant resurrection of Jesus. According to Mark Driscoll, "In total, the four Gospels, which

[k] Matt. 1:22–23.
[l] Isa. 7:14; 8:8.
[m] Gen. 17:8; Ex. 6:7; 25:8; 29:45–46; Lev. 22:33; 26:11–12; Deut. 4:20; 7:6; 14:2; 29:13; 1 Kings 6:13; Jer. 7:23; 11:4; 24:7; 30:22; 31:33; 32:38; Ezek. 11:20; 14:11; 36:28; 37:23, 27; Zech. 2:10; Matt. 1:22–23; 2 Cor. 6:16.
[n] Matt. 28:20.

faithfully record his life, devote roughly one-third of their content to the climactic final week of Jesus' life leading up to the cross."[14] With such an overwhelming emphasis on the atonement, on the redemptive suffering of Jesus Christ, the Gospels have been often described as crucifixion narratives with extended introductions.

The New Testament is brimming with descriptions of what God did for us through the cross of Christ:

> Jesus is presented as having paid the penalty for sin (Rom. 3:25–26; 6:23; Gal. 3:13). He died in place of sinners so that they might become God's righteousness (2 Cor. 5:21). He redeemed sinners through his blood (Eph. 1:7). He paid the price for sinners to go free (1 Cor. 6:20; Gal. 5:1). He won the victory over death and sin, sharing with believers the victory (1 Cor. 15:55–57) that he paraded in spectacular fashion by his cross (Col. 2:15). Peter's statement captures well the means and importance of Jesus' ministry of atonement: "He himself bore our sins in his body on the tree, so that we might die to sin and live for righteousness; by his wounds you have been healed" (1 Pet. 2:24).[15]

A central way that these Gospel narratives describe how God has dealt with sin is "penal substitutionary atonement."[16] On the cross, Jesus took our place and bore the wrath that we deserved: "The doctrine of penal substitution states that God gave himself in the person of his Son to suffer instead of us the death, punishment and curse due to fallen humanity as the penalty for sin."[17]

Jesus Paid Our Ransom

First, to free us from bondage, Jesus paid our ransom on the cross. In the Gospel of Mark, Jesus foretells his death three times in detail.[o]

[o] Mark 8:31; 9:31; 10:33–34.

After these predictions, Jesus says to his disciples in Mark 10:45, "For even the Son of Man came not to be served but to serve, and to give his life as a ransom for many." In other words, Jesus would serve and take the low place, humbling himself to die on the cross as a "ransom for many." In his death, Jesus paid the ransom price of his life as a substitutionary payment in the place of sinners.[18]

The New Testament writers frequently borrow the language of the Old Testament to describe the redemption secured by Jesus. Mark, in using the idea of a "ransom," is borrowing from the Old Testament imagery connected with the Exodus.[19] During his transfiguration, Luke tells us that Jesus "appeared in glory and spoke of his departure [literally "exodus"], which he was about to accomplish at Jerusalem."[20] Just like Moses, Christ would lead his people out of bondage. But Christ's deliverance would far surpass the work of Moses.[21]

Ransom is a major dimension of God's redemptive plan revealed in Scripture. According to theologian John Murray:

> The language of redemption is the language of purchase and more specifically of ransom. . . . Ransom presupposes some kind of bondage or captivity, and redemption, therefore, implies that from which the ransom secures us. . . . Redemption applies to every aspect in which we are bound, and it releases us into a liberty that is nothing less than the liberty of the glory of the children of God.[22]

In his letter to the Colossians, Paul says that we ought to give "thanks to the Father, who has qualified you to share in the inheritance of the saints in light. He has delivered us from the domain of darkness and transferred us to the kingdom of his beloved Son, in whom we have redemption, the forgiveness of sins."[p] Paul contrasts the condition sinners found themselves in apart from the gospel. We were in the "domain of darkness." We were citizens of Satan's dark kingdom. But in Christ, because of the cross, Paul says we have been brought out of this deadly kingdom into the life and light of the kingdom of God's beloved Son.

Bible scholar N. T. Wright notes that Paul borrows the salvation vocabulary of the exodus: "This is Exodus language. Just as the children of Israel were brought out of slavery under Pharaoh and were established as God's free people, so now, by the preaching of the gospel, people everywhere can be transferred from the grip of the powers into the kingdom of Jesus."[23] All those who have trusted in Christ and have been saved by him are partakers of a kingdom that includes the glorious inheritance of the saints in light.

This inheritance is described elsewhere as "imperishable, undefiled, and unfading, kept in heaven for you."[q] All of these spectacular blessings were purchased by Christ's redemption. This redemption has at its heart the forgiveness of sins: "You were ransomed from the futile ways inherited from your forefathers, not with perishable things such as silver or gold, but with the precious blood of Christ, like that of a lamb without blemish or spot."[24]

Peter, like Paul, saw the work of redemption purchased by Christ as a new exodus: "But you are a chosen race, a royal priesthood, a holy nation, a people for his own possession, that you may proclaim the excellencies of him who called you out of darkness into his marvelous light. Once you were not a people, but now you are God's people; once you had not received mercy, but now you have received mercy."[r]

---

[p] Col. 1:12–14.
[q] 1 Pet. 1:4.
[r] 1 Pet. 2:9–10.

Jesus Bore Our Curse

Jesus not only paid our ransom; Jesus also bore our curse. According to Paul, "Christ redeemed us from the curse of the law by becoming a curse for us—for it is written, 'Cursed is everyone who is hanged on a tree.'"[s] Christ became our curse bearer on the cross: "When Jesus emptied the cup of God's wrath, He endured the ultimate limit of the Law's curse. Christ became a curse for us. Literally, He became a curse in our place as our substitute. He experienced the full fury of the curse that we should have experienced."[25]

Part of the curse that Jesus bore for sinners was the God-forsakenness that he endured during the final hours of his crucifixion. According to Mark's Gospel: "And at the ninth hour Jesus cried with a loud voice, 'Eloi, Eloi, lema sabachthani?' which means, 'My God, my God, why have you forsaken me?'"[t]

J. I. Packer comments about this passage:

> On the cross Jesus lost all the good that he had before: all sense of his Father's presence and love, all sense of physical, mental, and spiritual well-being, all enjoyment of God and of created things, all ease and solace of friendship, were taken from him, and in their place was nothing but loneliness, pain, a killing sense of human malice and callousness, and a horror of great spiritual darkness.[26]

While the physical pain was excruciating, this paled in comparison to the mental and spiritual sufferings Jesus endured on Calvary. "What was packed into less than four hundred minutes was an eternity of agony."[27]

Christ endured the curse for us, and we receive all of heaven's

---

[s] Gal. 3:13.
[t] Mark 15:34.

spiritual blessings in him.[u] According to Jerry Bridges, "We should never cease to be amazed that the One who established the Law and determined its curse should Himself ransom us from that curse by bearing it in our place."[28] And Paul Zahl writes, "The one word of grace depends on the two words of God, law and grace, being related and reconciled in the crucifixion of Christ. Without the atonement, law would reign and grace would have no foundation."[29] Bearing our curse, Jesus fulfilled the promise of the suffering servant, who is also identified as the "man of sorrows" in Isaiah 53. "Jesus suffered the indignity of accusation and condemnation and the shame of crucifixion. His was the tortured soul in Gethsemane, the torn flesh at Calvary. And as thick darkness enveloped the whole land, it was He who was pierced for our transgressions and crushed for our iniquities; His was the punishment that brought us peace; His were the wounds that wrought our healing."[30]

Jesus Was Our Propitiation and Expiation

In Romans 3:21–26 Paul describes how God has completely and justly dealt with our sins and condemnation in a way that perfectly accords with his righteousness:

> But now the righteousness of God has been manifested apart from the law, although the Law and the Prophets bear witness to it—the righteousness of God through faith in Jesus Christ for all who believe. For there is no distinction: for all have sinned and fall short of the glory of God, and are justified by his grace as a gift, through the redemption that is in Christ Jesus, whom God put forward as a propitiation by his blood, to be received by faith. This was to show God's righteousness, because in his divine forbearance he had passed over former sins. It was to

[u] Eph. 1:3.

> show his righteousness at the present time, so that he might be just and the justifier of the one who has faith in Jesus.

God's wrath is his holy hostility toward sin and his just anger toward anything that violates his holiness. It is his righteous reaction against unrighteousness. God's holy and righteous wrath should be justly poured out on all of humanity. According to Packer: "The wrath of God is as personal, and as potent, as his love; and, just as the blood-shedding of the Lord Jesus was the direct manifesting of his Father's love toward us, so it was the direct averting of his Father's wrath against us."[31]

In Christ, God has made a way possible for both his grace and his righteousness to be displayed in the salvation of sinners. God did this by putting Christ forward as a "propitiation by his blood."[v] According to John Murray, the doctrine of propitiation is precisely this:

> That God loved the objects of His wrath so much that He gave His own Son to the end that He by His blood should make provision for the removal of His wrath. It was Christ's so to deal with the wrath that the loved would no longer be the objects of wrath, and love would achieve its aim of making the children of wrath the children of God's good pleasure.[32]

The book of Hebrews also emphasizes both the propitiation and expiation that Jesus secured through his work as both high priest and sacrifice. The imagery that Christ was "made . . . sin" for us[w] and that he "bore our sins"[x] matches the role of both goats on the Day of Atonement—the one sacrificed as a sin offering and

[v] Rom. 3:24–25.
[w] 2 Cor. 5:21.
[x] 1 Pet. 2:24.

the one that carried off the confessed sins of the people. In his death, "the Lord has laid on him the iniquity of us all."[y] In Psalm 51:1–2 we read:

> Have mercy on me, O God,
> according to your steadfast love;
> according to your abundant mercy
> blot out my transgressions.
> Wash me thoroughly from my iniquity,
> and cleanse me from my sin!

The Day of Atonement was a foreshadowing of Jesus, the Lamb of God who takes away the sins of the world, and our Great High Priest who is able to sympathize with us in our weaknesses. These great images of the priest, slaughter, and scapegoat are all given by God to help us more fully comprehend Jesus's bloody sacrifice for us on the cross. Jesus's fulfillment of the Day of Atonement is why we are forgiven for and cleansed from our sins. Regarding the centrality of sacrifice for atonement, Charles Spurgeon writes: "Many pretend to keep the atonement, and yet they tear the bowels out of it. They profess to believe in the gospel, but it is a gospel without the blood of the atonement; and a bloodless gospel is a lifeless gospel, a dead gospel, and a damning gospel."[33] Jesus Christ fulfills and accomplishes forever what the two goats symbolized. The Old Testament sacrifice of animals has been replaced by the perfect sacrifice of Christ.[z] Christ paid sin's penalty.[aa] He redeemed us,[ab] paying the price that sets us free.[ac] He turned away God's wrath[ad] and reconciled

---

[y] Isa. 53:6.
[z] Heb. 9:26; 10:5–10; 1 John 2:1–2; 4:9–10.
[aa] Rom. 3:25–26; 6:23; Gal 3:13.
[ab] Eph. 1:7.
[ac] 1 Cor. 6:20; Gal. 5:1.
[ad] Rom. 3:25.

believers to God[ae] so we can be forgiven for our sins and cleansed from all unrighteousness.[af]

First John 1:9 refers to propitiation and expiation: "If we confess our sins, he is faithful and just to forgive us our sins and to cleanse us from all unrighteousness." Elsewhere in 1 John, the work of Jesus is said to "cleanse us from all sin"[ag] and to be "the propitiation for our sins."[ah]

Jesus Was Our Substitute

In Romans 5:6–11, Paul describes how the salvation of sinners is not only by propitiation but also by substitution. That is, Jesus Christ became a substitute and died in our place for our sins. At the cross, God, once and for all time, demonstrated his love for us. God provides evidence through action of his love for sinners: "God shows his love for us in that while we were still sinners, Christ died for us."[ai] Notice the tense of the verb: "God shows." The death of Christ in the past proves today, tomorrow, and for all time that God loves us. The death of Christ is a timeless proof of God's love. Throughout the endless ages of eternity, forgiven sinners will sing the glories of the Lamb who was slain for them on Calvary. The cross is the supreme display of God's love.

The cross is the public display not only of God's righteousness[aj] but also of God's love.[ak] And Paul makes clear in this passage that there is no love that has ever been that can compare to the dying love of Christ for sinners. Paul's words "Christ died for us" in Romans 5:8 are even more amazing when you observe how he

[ae] Eph. 2:16.
[af] 1 John 1:9.
[ag] 1 John 1:7.
[ah] 1 John 2:2.
[ai] Rom. 5:8.
[aj] Rom. 3:21.
[ak] Rom. 5:8.

has described "us." In the context, the "us" is described as "weak,"[al] "ungodly,"[am] "sinners,"[an] and "enemies."[ao] This is astounding. While we were helpless, ungodly, wicked, sinners, and enemies of God, Christ died for us.

Christ died in place of his enemies. He died in our place for our sins. Paul says this in another way in Romans 4:25: Jesus "was delivered up for our trespasses." In other words, Jesus was handed over for our sins. This was only possible because Jesus didn't have any sins: "For our sake he made him to be sin who knew no sin, so that in him we might become the righteousness of God."[ap]

Salvation and Obedience

The work of Jesus was not just his death on the cross but also his perfect life. His death accomplished the forgiveness of our sins and removed the guilt and stain of sins, securing assurance of eternal life. Our sins were imputed (attributed) to Christ, and he died the death of a sinner. However, his righteousness was imputed to those who have faith in Christ. Francis Turretin explains the significance of Christ's obedience:

> The obedience of Christ has a twofold efficacy, satisfactory and meritorious; the former by which we are freed from the punishments incurred by sin; the latter by which (through the remission of sin) a right to eternal life and salvation is acquired for us. For as sin has brought upon us two evils—the loss of life and exposure to death—so redemption must procure the two opposite benefits—deliverance from death and a right to life, escape from hell and an entrance into heaven.[34]

[al] Rom. 5:6.
[am] Rom. 5:6.
[an] Rom. 5:8.
[ao] Rom. 5:10.
[ap] 2 Cor. 5:21.

The benefits of Christ's righteousness are proclaimed in Romans 5:18–19: "Therefore, as one trespass led to condemnation for all men, so one act of righteousness leads to justification and life for all men. For as by the one man's disobedience the many were made sinners, so by the one man's obedience the many will be made righteous." John Calvin explains how Christ's obedience is the ground for our pardon: "To justify therefore, is nothing else than to acquit from the charge of guilt, as if innocence were proved. Hence, when God justifies us through the intercession of Christ, he does not acquit us on a proof of our own innocence, but by an imputation of righteousness, so that though not righteous in ourselves, we are deemed righteous in Christ."[35]

Not only are believers delivered from condemnation and exempted from eternal death because of his death, but they are also deemed worthy of reward and declared righteous because of Christ's sinless life. His purity is imputed to us and we are declared and judged righteous "in order that the righteous requirement of the law might be fulfilled in us."[aq]

The work of Christ is a fulfillment of Isaiah 61:10: "I will greatly rejoice in the LORD; my soul shall exult in my God, for he has clothed me with the garments of salvation; he has covered me with the robe of righteousness." Jonathan Edwards writes: "Christ's perfect obedience shall be reckoned to our account so that we shall have the benefit of it, as though we had performed it ourselves: and so we suppose that a title to eternal life is given us as the reward of this righteousness."[36]

Jesus did not just come that our sins would be removed, but he also came that we might receive his righteousness, which was only possible after the debt for our sin had been paid: "For our sake

---

[aq] Rom. 8:4.

he made him to be sin who knew no sin, so that in him we might become the righteousness of God."[ar] Martin Luther called this "the great exchange":

> That is the mystery which is rich in divine grace to sinners: wherein by a wonderful exchange our sins are no longer ours but Christ's and the righteousness of Christ not Christ's but ours. He has emptied Himself of his righteousness that He might clothe us with it, and fill us with it. And He has taken our evils upon Himself that He might deliver us from them . . . in the same manner as He grieved and suffered in our sins, and was confounded, in the same manner we rejoice and glory in His righteousness.[37]

The benefit of this is reconciliation and a new identity.

In Colossians 1:21–22 we read an amazing promise: "And you, who once were alienated and hostile in mind, doing evil deeds, he has now reconciled in his body of flesh by his death, in order to present you holy and blameless and above reproach before him." Notice the words, "holy," "blameless," and "above reproach." These descriptive words are usually used in reference to Jesus Christ. But now, because of what Jesus Christ has done for us, paying the penalty of sins, we can now stand holy, blameless, and above reproach before God our creator. By faith we are "in Christ" and as such we are seen as he is. Because of faith in Christ, you are the righteousness of God.

Jesus Gave Us Access to God

By his death and resurrection, Jesus becomes our way to God. His death is the sacrifice for us. He is the Lamb of God who takes away your sins, but he is also your priest. In the Old Testament, the priest represented God to the people and the people back to God. But now

[ar] 2 Cor. 5:21.

Jesus is your high priest. Being both God and man, he fulfills the role of priest perfectly. The temple was where God was present, but in the temple was a veil that separated sinful humans from the presence of the holy God. But in Jesus, humanity had the most personal presence of God possible. He was called "Immanuel," meaning "God with us." Jesus called himself the temple of God. And when Jesus died, the veil in the temple—the barrier between God and us—was torn in two from top to bottom. This means that God tore his own temple veil and made himself accessible to us through the death of Jesus.

First Timothy 2:5 calls Jesus the only mediator between God and humanity. Hebrews refers to Jesus twice as the mediator of the new covenant.[as] In Jesus you have unbridled and unhindered access to God. You can now approach God without fear of judgment and with boldness.[at] God has made himself accessible. Jesus, the "great high priest," has enabled you to "draw near to the throne of grace" of the Father with "confidence."[au] No longer do you have to hold your head in shame in prayer, but you can come to the Father with Christ-centered confidence.

Jesus Rose from Death and Conquered Our Enemy

Much of the focus so far has been on the cross as God's gracious response to our own sinful and willful irresponsibility, choices, and actions. This is because we are perpetrators of evil—and this is what separates us from God. It is this aspect of sin that has been dealt with by the vicarious sacrifice theme of the atonement.

However, we are also victims of evil and have enemies who harm us. We are victims who have been sinned against in numerous ways. Because of sins done to us, we are also captive, held in

[as] Heb. 9:15; 12:24.
[at] Eph. 3:12.
[au] Heb. 4:16.

bondage by powers in some sense external to us and greater than we are. Or we may be held in bondage to our own desires or fears, our self-centeredness or despair. Sometimes the Bible describes the human problem as suffering, being in bondage, slavery, or captivity, each and all of which separate us from God.

What we need in this regard is for God to fight on our behalf, against our enemy, for our freedom from bondage. This is what God did in the exodus for his people. The clearest and most powerful manifestation of God doing this for us is Christ's victory over death in the resurrection.[av] In this victory over principalities, powers, and death, the Son reclaims creation for the Father and freedom for you. "He disarmed the rulers and authorities and put them to open shame, by triumphing over them in him."[aw]

In answering the question, "How does Christ's resurrection benefit us?" the Heidelberg Catechism answers: "First, by his resurrection he has overcome death, so that he might make us share in the righteousness he won for us by his death. Second, by his power we too are already now resurrected to a new life. Third, Christ's resurrection is a guarantee of our glorious resurrection."

God accomplished redemption in Christ's victory over sin and death, but the effects of that victory have yet to be fully realized. So while the ultimate outcome has been assured,[ax] the struggle between life and death, good and evil, continues. However, the *shalom*, freedom, and rest of redemption will one day be fully realized, when Jesus returns.

Jesus was physically raised from death as "the firstborn from the dead,"[ay] securing a future resurrection like his own for all those who are united to him through faith. Mark Driscoll writes:

[av] Eph. 1:19–20.
[aw] Col. 2:15.
[ax] Rom. 8:18–21; 1 Cor. 15:51–57; Revelation 21.
[ay] Col. 1:18.

> Jesus' resurrection is the precedent and pattern of our own: "Christ has been raised from the dead, the firstfruits of those who have fallen asleep" [1 Cor. 15:20]. As his body was resurrected in complete health, so too will we rise and never experience pain, injury, or death ever again. This is because through the resurrection, Jesus has put death to death.[38]

Through his triumphant resurrection, Jesus opened the way for us to experience resurrection and eternal life in the new earth when he returns, instead of the death we deserve.

Christ's victory gives us back our identity and restores our meaning. We recognize, and may truly know for the first time, that we have a future that ends in peace, as well as a past that can be healed and forgiven, and now live in the hope of the gospel. Christ opens up for us a new identity because he himself remained always true to his identity, a share of which he offers to us.

In Christ's victory, fear and shame are banished, to be replaced by profound joy that we are no longer strangers to God and to one another, that we are no longer so utterly isolated and alone. Robert Sherman writes: "Liberation from the bondage of our past and yearning for a fulfilled future find their realization in Christ's reclaiming of the creation."[39]

Our Future Salvation

The blessings of Christ's work will be enjoyed by all of the redeemed into the ages of eternity. Paul writes:

> God, being rich in mercy, because of the great love with which he loved us, even when we were dead in our trespasses, made us alive together with Christ—by grace you have been saved—and raised us up with him and seated us with him in the heavenly places in Christ Jesus, so that in the coming ages he might show

> the immeasurable riches of his grace in kindness toward us in Christ Jesus.[az]

One of the purposes of God's redemptive work for us in Christ was to demonstrate the riches of his grace for all eternity.[40]

For this reason, it is helpful to understand more fully the implications of the atonement for the age to come. According to Yarbrough:

> "Atonement" may be defined as God's work on sinners' behalf to reconcile them to himself. It is the divine activity that confronts and resolves the problem of human sin so that people may enjoy full fellowship with God both now and in the age to come. While in one sense the meaning of atonement is as broad and diverse as all of God's saving work throughout time and eternity, in another it is as particular and restricted as the crucifixion of Jesus. For in the final analysis Scripture presents his sacrificial death as the central component of God's reconciling mercy. This explains why Revelation 22:3, for example, shows not only God but also the Lamb—slain to atone for sin—occupying the throne of heaven in the age to come.[41]

The new heavens and the new earth described in Revelation 21:1–6 are a picture of perfection:

> Then I saw a new heaven and a new earth, for the first heaven and the first earth had passed away, and the sea was no more. And I saw the holy city, new Jerusalem, coming down out of heaven from God, prepared as a bride adorned for her husband. And I heard a loud voice from the throne saying, "Behold, the dwelling place of God is with man. He will dwell with them, and they will be his people, and God himself will be with them

[az] Eph. 2:4–7.

> as their God. He will wipe away every tear from their eyes, and death shall be no more, neither shall there be mourning, nor crying, nor pain anymore, for the former things have passed away." And he who was seated on the throne said, "Behold, I am making all things new." Also he said, "Write this down, for these words are trustworthy and true." And he said to me, "It is done! I am the Alpha and the Omega, the beginning and the end. To the thirsty I will give from the spring of the water of life without payment."

Revelation 21 describes a world reborn, a new creation where everything we lost in the fall is regained. This vision of a new creation,[ba] a new heaven and a new earth after judgment, reminds us of God's promise to Noah to make all things new despite sin. The covenantal refrain repeated in Exodus is also fulfilled in the new creation—"They will be his people, and God himself will be with them."[bb] Immanuel, "God with us," is not just about the incarnation but is the eternal presence. The final home for believers will not be a disembodied heaven but rather a fully glorified and bodied existence in the new heaven and the new earth. It won't just be Eden restored, but rather it will be a whole new world reborn, a place where the curse is completely and totally reversed! Death will be replaced by life.[bc] Night will be replaced by light.[bd] The light of the world will be the light of heaven! Corruption will be replaced by purity.[be] Disgrace will be replaced by grace.

God himself will dwell with his people, in his perfect place, and will bless his people with his presence. Forever. The chief reason why this place will be perfect is that believers will be in the presence of

---

[ba] Rev. 21:1.
[bb] Rev. 21:3.
[bc] Rev. 21:4.
[bd] Rev. 21:23–25.
[be] Rev. 21:27.

Almighty God. God will once again dwell with his people, and we will see him face-to-face![bf] Faith will give way to sight and prayer to praise. Sin and violence will be ultimately and finally replaced by *shalom*.

Our eyes will be fixed upon the Lamb of God, slain for sinners, who occupies the throne of God. John calls Jesus "Lamb" twenty-eight times in the book of Revelation.[bg] This is a clear reference to the sacrifices of Passover and the Day of Atonement. This Lamb is also on a throne, symbolizing that he is victorious king. John tells us that Jesus conquered by suffering and dying on the cross. He shed his blood to cleanse his people from their sins.

Christopher Wright explains that the work of Jesus restores the peace that was vandalized in Genesis 3:

> And the river and tree of life, from which humanity had been barred in the earliest chapters of the Bible's grand narrative, will, in its final chapter, provide the healing of the nations which the narrative has longed for ever since the scattering of Babel (Rev. 22:2). The curse will be gone from the whole of creation (Rev. 22:3). The earth will be filled with the glory of God and all the nations of humanity will walk in His light (Rev. 21:24). Such is the glorious climax of the Bible's grand narrative.[42]

The Gospel and *Hesed*

In the Bible, suffering is regarded as an intrusion into this created world. Creation was made good.[bh] When sin entered, suffering also entered in the form of conflict, pain, corruption, drudgery, and death.[bi] The work of Christ is to deliver us from suffering, corrup-

[bf] Rev. 22:4.
[bg] Rev. 5:6, 8, 12ff.; 6:1, 16; 7:9ff., 14, 17; 8:1; 12:11; 13:8; 14:1, 4, 10; 15:3; 17:14; 19:7, 9; 21:9, 14, 22ff.; 22:1, 3.
[bh] Gen. 1:31.
[bi] Gen. 3:15–19.

tion, and death,[bj] as well as from sin.[bk] In the new heaven and the new earth, suffering has been finally abolished.[bl]

In the gospel of Jesus Christ, God demonstrates that he is for us and not against us. Everything we have as believers has been granted to us because of what Jesus has already done for us. According to D. A. Carson:

> Everything that is coming to us from God comes through Christ Jesus. Christ Jesus has won our pardon; He has reconciled us to God; He has canceled our sin; He has secured the gift of the Spirit for us; He has granted eternal life to us and promises us the life of the consummation; He has made us children of the new covenant; His righteousness has been accounted as ours; He has risen from the dead, and all of God's sovereignty is mediated through Him and directed to our good and to God's glory. This is the Son whom God sent to redeem us. In God's all-wise plan and all-powerful action, all these blessings have been won by His Son's odious death and triumphant resurrection. All the blessings God has for us are tied up with the work of Christ.[43]

And all of these blessings are freely yours in Jesus Christ. Now and forever. All by grace. Grace is available because Jesus went through the valley of the shadow of death and rose from death. The gospel engages our life with all its pain, shame, rejection, lostness, sin, and death. So now, to your pain the gospel says, "You will be healed." To your shame the gospel says, "You can now come to God in confidence." To your rejection the gospel says, "You are accepted!" To your lostness the gospel says, "You are found, and I won't ever let you go." To your sin the gospel says, "You are forgiven and God

[bj] Rom. 8:21; 1 Cor. 15:26.
[bk] Matt. 1:21.
[bl] Rev. 21:4; cf. Isa. 65:17ff.

declares you pure and righteous." To your death the gospel says, "You once were dead, but now you are alive."

Because of his finished work, anyone who trusts in Jesus Christ can have this comfort in life and in death:

> That I am not my own, but belong—body and soul, in life and in death—to my faithful Savior Jesus Christ. He has fully paid for all my sins with his precious blood, and has set me free from the tyranny of the devil. He also watches over me in such a way that not a hair can fall from my head without the will of my Father in heaven: in fact, all things must work together for my salvation. Because I belong to him, Christ, by his Holy Spirit, assures me of eternal life and makes me wholeheartedly willing and ready from now on to live for him.[44]

The gospel of Jesus Christ is the fulfillment of God's *hesed*—God's steadfast love that endures forever.

Chapter 5

It's Grace All the Way

From Jesus Christ "we have all received grace upon grace."[a] We are saved solely through faith in Jesus Christ because of God's grace and Christ's merit alone. We are neither saved by our merits nor declared righteous by our good works. We do not deserve grace, or else it wouldn't be grace. This means that God grants salvation not because of the good things we do or even because of our faith—and despite our sin. This is the ring of liberation in the Christian proclamation. If it is not grace all the way, then we will spend our lifetime wondering if we have done enough to get that total acceptance for which we desperately long. "I said the prayer, but did I say it passionately enough?" "I repented, but was it sincere enough?" Election puts salvation in the only place that it can possibly exist: God's hands. God's election is the unconditional and unmerited nature of his grace.

Ephesians 2:4–5 proclaims Gods grace clearly: "God, being rich in mercy, because of the great love with which he loved us, even when we were dead in trespasses, made us alive together with Christ—by grace have you been saved." Regeneration (being made

[a] John 1:16.

spiritually alive) takes place when we as spiritually dead people are made alive in Christ. Dead people do not cooperate with grace. Unless regeneration takes place first, there is no possibility of faith. Paul got this from Jesus, who told Nicodemus: "Unless a man is born again first, he cannot possibly see or enter the kingdom of God."[b]

The Bible teaches us that new birth (regeneration) precedes saving faith in Christ. In other words, God in his sovereign grace makes spiritually dead people alive so they can have faith in Christ and be justified. Spiritual death is human self-dependence. When we are made alive, we are able for the first time ever to place our hope in someone else.

Left to our own abilities, we don't cooperate with grace or even seek God.[c] We choose ourselves over God every time. We are unable to seek God because we're spiritually dead. Just as Lazarus couldn't raise himself from the dead, we can't raise ourselves from spiritual death. We also need Jesus to say, "Lazarus, come out."

This teaching makes God's grace even more amazing. Salvation belongs to the Lord.[d] It is not something we do, enact, or achieve. Jesus loves us, and he draws us to himself for God's glory while we are spiritually dead and utterly undeserving. That is grace, indeed. That is liberation.

As humans, we inherited a nature and a will that are in bondage to sin from Adam. This is why Augustine argued, "What God's grace has not freed will not be free."[1] Calvin said it another way: "Human will does not by liberty obtain grace, but by grace obtains liberty."[2]

We are born in sin. We are naturally enemies of God and lovers of evil. We needed to be made alive (regenerated) so that we could even have faith in Christ. All of this is grace that we don't

[b] See John 3:3.
[c] Rom. 3:11.
[d] Ps. 3:8, Jon. 2:9.

deserve. When we realize we don't earn or attain this grace, we also realize we cannot lose it. God graciously preserves us and keeps us. When we are faithless toward him, he is still faithful.[e] The grace just keeps going.

But if the gospel is outside of us, if we can't even stand before God until he graciously attributes to us the righteousness of Jesus Christ and attributes to him on the cross the consequences of our sin, how can this be so liberating? Is it really good news if our freedom is won by the hand of another? The fact that we try to reserve just a little part of salvation to ourselves is evidence that we don't understand our slavery. We look for our righteousness in some action or quality of ourselves—no matter how little. When grace opens our eyes we realize our righteousness is outside of us. It is then that we realize just how glorious, unchanging, and enduring the righteousness of Jesus (now ours!) actually is.

This good news is illustrated in John Bunyan's spiritual autobiography, *Grace Abounding to the Chief of Sinners*:

> Every little touch would hurt my conscience. But one day, as I was passing in the field, suddenly I thought of a sentence: "Your righteousness is in heaven." With the eyes of faith, I saw Jesus sitting at God's right hand. And I suddenly realized—THERE is my righteousness. Wherever I was, or whatever I was doing, God could not say to me, "where is your righteousness?" for that was right before Him. I saw that my good frame of heart could not make my righteousness better nor a bad frame could not make my righteousness worse. My righteousness was in Jesus Christ Himself, forever!
>
> Now my chains fell off indeed. I felt delivered from slavery to guilt and fears. I went home rejoicing for the love and graces of God. Now I could look from myself to him. . . . Christ is my

[e] 2 Tim. 2:13.

> treasure, my righteousness. Christ was my wisdom, righteousness, holiness, and salvation.[3]

Ephesians 2:8–10 teaches all this clearly: "For by grace you have been saved through faith. And this is not your own doing; it is the gift of God, not a result of works, so that no one may boast. For we are his workmanship, created in Christ Jesus for good works, which God prepared beforehand, that we should walk in them." We are saved by grace alone,[4] through faith alone.[5]

Ephesians 2 is filled with the high-octane gospel of grace for both our justification and sanctification. It begins with how believers were dead in their sins, then moves to how God loved us and rescued us from this death by his grace, bringing salvation to all in Christ, uniting Jews and Gentiles as one people in which the Spirit of God dwells. The first half of the chapter focuses on God's rescue operation for his people, which delivered us from our sin and God's wrath, and ends with verse 10, which centers on how God's deliverance means we are created anew for lives of righteousness. As one commentator notes, salvation has already been described by Paul as "a resurrection from the dead, a liberation from slavery, and a rescue from condemnation"; he moves now to the idea of a new creation.[6]

The theme of Ephesians 2:8–9 is clear: grace. This theme was already mentioned in Ephesians 2:5, but what was then more of an "undercurrent" now becomes the main point.[7] We are saved by grace, not by anything we have done. The passage is a traditional one used to support the idea that justification before God is by grace alone, not by anything we do.[8] And for good reason. The verses strike with great emphasis the note of salvation as a complete "gift of God." We have done *nothing* to bring it about that could lead us to boast about it.[9] And yet it is nearly impossible *not* to boast in the radical love of God when we grasp this reality.

We now move to Ephesians 2:10 with its focus on "good works." It is tempting at first glance to think that verses 8 and 9 are about grace and verse 10 is about works. But this would be to miss something very important that we easily neglect: everything is grace. Or, as one scholar puts it, "it is grace all the way."[10] But what does that mean exactly?

Ephesians has focused on the work of God from the very beginning, in 1:1. Now it all "comes to a crescendo."[11] Notice how God-centered Ephesians 2:10 is. In the Greek, the first word in the sentence is "his," which is an unusual placement and puts the emphasis squarely on God. We are "*his* workmanship." We "*are created* [by God] in Christ Jesus" for good works. These good works are those "that *God* prepared beforehand." Clearly, works are important to Paul, but his emphasis here is on *God* bringing them about within us.

Notice that this verse does three important things.[12] First, it gives the reason *why* Paul can say in verses 8 and 9 that salvation is a complete gift of God: we are *his* workmanship, re-created in Jesus Christ.[13] Second, it points forward to other places the new creation idea is found in Ephesians.[f] Third, it completes the section of Ephesians 2:1–10 in a fitting way by using again the idea of "walking," which contrasts with Ephesians 2:2 where Paul talks about how we used to "walk" in sin, following the "course of the world." Now we "walk" in good works God has set before us.

Ephesians 2:10 continues that we have been created in Christ Jesus "for good works." So we are saved *for the purpose of* walking in good works. Good works are never the ground or cause of our salvation. They can't be; they just don't work like that. They are not the cause but the "*goal* of the new creation."[14] And God has already prepared them for us ahead of time.

---

[f]Eph. 2:14–15; 4:24.

We must always hold Ephesians 2:10 together with 2:8–9. The Bible paints a holistic picture of the believer as one whose life is continually lived in grace that bears fruit, fruit that is used by God to bless others.

How do we then live? If our works are "prepared beforehand," what do we do? Paul says we "walk in them." We show up. We abide in the vine of Jesus.[g] We walk by the Spirit.[h] We do our best not to muck it up. But we will; and when we do, grace picks us up again. It's like the old Rich Mullins lyric: "If I stand, let me stand on the promise that you will see me through, and if I can't, let me fall on the grace that first brought me to you." There is a damaging idea floating around that says, "God saved you, now what are you going to do for him?" This is a recipe for failure. If you come to the table believing you can do anything for God in your own strength or repay him on any level, you have already lost. You are back to confessing your self-dependent spiritual death from which Jesus saved you.

Above all else and before any discussion of what we should *do*, we must understand deeply in our bones who we *are*: the workmanship of God. You are his project. So, you are invited to be who you are. Your life is not your own; it was bought with a price. Live with the gratitude, humility, joy, and peace that come from knowing it does not all depend on you. You are loved and accepted in Christ, so you don't have to focus on what you do or don't do for God. Now you can focus on what Jesus has done for you, and that will cause you to love God more. Then you can't help but walk in grace, realizing how costly God's grace was.

Our salvation cost God the precious blood of Christ. Dietrich Bonhoeffer writes that God's grace "is costly grace because it cost

[g] John 15:4.
[h] Gal. 5:16–25.

God the life of His Son. . . . God did not reckon His Son too dear a price to pay for our life, but delivered him up for us."[15] God accomplished all he intended through his Son. God gave everything in Jesus. This is why Jesus said: "The Son of Man came . . . to give his life as a ransom for many."[i] Paul uses the language of ransom: you were bought at a price.[j]

Steve Brown tells a story about costly grace and freedom.[16] Abraham Lincoln went to a slave auction one day and was appalled at what he saw. He was drawn to a young woman on the auction block. The bidding began, and Lincoln bid until he purchased her—no matter the cost. After he paid the auctioneer, he walked over to the woman and said "You're free." "Free? What is that supposed to mean?" she asked. "It means you are free," Lincoln answered, "completely free!" "Does it mean I can do whatever I want to do?" "Yes," he said, "free to do whatever you want to do." "Free to say whatever I want to say?" "Yes, free to say whatever you want to say." "Does freedom mean," asking with hope and hesitation, "that I can go wherever I want to go?" "It means exactly that. That you can go wherever you want to go." With tears of joy and gratitude welling up in her eyes, she said, "Then, I think I'll go with you."

This story illustrates what God did for us. We are bought with a price and it was costly—the life of God's own Son. Once our new master paid the price for us, he set us free.

Charles Wesley reflects this freedom in his hymn "And Can It Be That I Should Gain?":

Long my imprisoned spirit lay,
Fast bound in sin and nature's night;

---

[i] Matt. 20:28.
[j] 1 Cor. 7:23.

Thine eye diffused a quickening ray.
I woke, the dungeon flamed with light;
My chains fell off, my heart was free,
I rose, went forth, and followed thee.
My chains fell off, my heart was free,
I rose, went forth, and followed thee.

"My chains fell off, my heart was free. I rose, went forth, and followed thee." You go where you are loved. And we love God only because he first loved us. You don't need to be exhorted and told "You'd better love God." How could you not? You've been ransomed by God's grace.

Christians live every day by the grace of God. We receive forgiveness according to the riches of divine grace, and grace drives our sanctification. Paul tells us, "The grace of God has appeared, bringing salvation for all people, training us to renounce ungodliness and worldly passions, and to live self-controlled, upright, and godly lives."[k] This doesn't happen overnight; we "grow in the grace and knowledge of our Lord and Savior Jesus Christ."[l] Grace transforms our desires, motivations, and behavior.

In fact, God's grace grounds and empowers everything in the Christian life. Grace is the basis for:[17]

- Our Christian identity: "By the grace of God I am what I am."[m]
- Our standing before God: " . . . this grace in which we stand."[n]
- Our behavior: "We behaved in the world . . . by the grace of God."[o]

[k] Titus 2:11–12.
[l] 2 Pet. 3:18.
[m] 1 Cor. 15:10.
[n] Rom. 5:2.
[o] 2 Cor. 1:12.

- Our living: those who receive "the abundance of grace and the free gift of righteousness reign in life through the one man Jesus Christ,"[p] by the "grace of life."[q]
- Our holiness: God "called us to a holy calling . . . because of his own purpose and grace."[r]
- Our strength for living: "Be strengthened by the grace that is in Jesus Christ,"[s] for "it is good for the heart to be strengthened by grace."[t]
- Our way of speaking: "Let your speech always be gracious."[u]
- Our serving: "Serve one another, as good stewards of God's varied grace."[v]
- Our sufficiency: "My grace is sufficient for you."[w] "God is able to make all grace abound to you, so that having all sufficiency in all things at all times, you may abound in every good work."[x]
- Our response to difficulty and suffering: We get "grace to help in time of need,"[y] and when "you have suffered a little while, the God of all grace . . . will himself restore, confirm, strengthen, and establish you."[z]
- Our participation in God's mission: As recipients of grace we are privileged to serve as agents of grace. Believers receive grace,[aa] are encouraged to continue in grace,[ab] and are called to testify to the grace of God.[ac] In John 20:21 Jesus says, "As

[p] Rom. 5:17.
[q] 1 Pet. 3:7.
[r] 2 Tim. 1:9.
[s] 2 Tim. 2:1.
[t] Heb. 13:9.
[u] Col. 4:6.
[v] 1 Pet. 4:10.
[w] 2 Cor. 12:9.
[x] 2 Cor. 9:8.
[y] Heb. 4:16.
[z] 1 Pet. 5:10.
[aa] Acts 11:23.
[ab] Acts 13:43.
[ac] Acts 20:24.

the Father has sent me, even so I am sending you." God's mission is to the entire world.[18]

- Our future: God and his grace are everlasting. "Set your hope fully on the grace that will be brought to you at the revelation of Jesus Christ."[ad]
- Our hope beyond death: "Grace [reigns] through righteousness leading to eternal life through Jesus Christ our Lord."[ae]

This is liberation, indeed.

The gospel is all about God's grace through Jesus Christ. That's why Paul calls it "the gospel of the grace of God"[af] and "the word of his grace."[ag]

The gospel of the grace of God is the message everyone needs. The word of grace is proclaimed from every page of the Bible and ultimately revealed in Jesus Christ. The last verse of the Bible summarizes the message from Genesis to Revelation: "The grace of the Lord Jesus be with all."[ah] Because of and from Jesus "we have all received grace upon grace"[ai]—the gratuitous and undomesticated grace of God.

> The grace of the Lord Jesus Christ and the love of God and the fellowship of the Holy Spirit be with you all.[aj]

[ad] 1 Pet. 1:13.
[ae] Rom. 5:21.
[af] Acts 20:24.
[ag] Acts 14:3; 20:32; cf. Col. 1:5–6.
[ah] Rev. 22:21.
[ai] John 1:16.
[aj] 2 Cor. 13:14.

Concluding Prayer: "Wave upon Wave of Grace"

O God of grace, teach me to know that grace precedes, accompanies, and follows my salvation; that it sustains the redeemed soul, that not one link of its chain can ever break.
From Calvary's cross, wave upon wave of grace
reaches me,
deals with my sin,
washes me clean,
renews my heart,
strengthens my will,
draws out my affection,
kindles a flame in my soul,
rules throughout my inner man,
consecrates my every thought, word, work,
teaches me your immeasurable love.
How great are my privileges in Christ Jesus.
Without him I stand far off, a stranger, an outcast;
in him I draw near and touch His kingly scepter.
Without him I dare not lift up my guilty eyes;
in him I gaze upon my Father-God and friend.
Without him I hide my lips in trembling shame;

in him I open my mouth in petition and praise.
Without him all is wrath and consuming fire;
in him is all love, and the repose of my soul.
Without him is gaping hell below me, and eternal anguish;
in him its gates are barred to me by His precious blood!
Without him darkness spreads its horrors before me;
in him an eternity of glory is my boundless horizon.
Without him all within me is terror and dismay,
in him every accusation is charmed into joy and peace.
Without him all things external call for my condemnation;
in him they minister to my comfort,
and are to be enjoyed with thanksgiving.
Praise be to you for grace,
and for the unspeakable gift of Jesus.[1]

Appendix

The Grace of God in the Bible

The content for this appendix comes from Dane Ortlund.[1] He wrote a masterful article illustrating how God's grace is traced throughout the Bible.

Certain motifs course through the Scriptures from start to end, tying the whole thing together into a coherent tapestry—kingdom, temple, people of God, creation/new creation, and so on. Looking at every book of the Bible, Dane Ortlund argues that underneath and undergirding all of these is the motif of God's grace, his favor and love to the undeserving.

Genesis shows God's grace to a universally wicked world as he enters into relationship with a sinful family line (Abraham) and promises to bless the world through him.

Exodus shows God's grace to his enslaved people in bringing them out of Egyptian bondage.

Leviticus shows God's grace in providing his people with a sacrificial system to atone for their sins.

Numbers shows God's grace in patiently sustaining his grumbling people in the wilderness and bringing them to the border of the Promised Land, not because of them but in spite of them.

Deuteronomy shows God's grace in giving the people the new land "not because of your righteousness" (chap. 9).

Joshua shows God's grace in giving Israel victory after victory in their conquest of the land with neither superior numbers nor superior obedience on Israel's part.

Judges shows God's grace in taking sinful, weak Israelites as leaders and using them to purge the land, time and again, of foreign incursion and idolatry.

Ruth shows God's grace in incorporating a poverty-stricken, desolate, foreign woman into the line of Christ.

1 and 2 Samuel show God's grace in establishing the throne (forever—2 Samuel 7) of an adulterous murderer.

1 and 2 Kings show God's grace in repeatedly prolonging the exacting of justice and judgment for kingly sin "for the sake of" David. (And remember: by the ancient hermeneutical presupposition of corporate solidarity, by which the one stands for the many and the many for the one, the king represented the people; the people were *in* their king; as the king went, so went they.)

1 and 2 Chronicles show God's grace by continually reassuring the returning exiles of God's self-initiated promises to David and his sons.

Ezra shows God's grace to Israel in working through the most powerful pagan ruler of the time (Cyrus) to bring his people back home to a rebuilt temple.

Nehemiah shows God's grace in providing for the rebuilding of the walls of the city that represented the heart of God's promises to his people.

Esther shows God's grace in protecting his people from a Persian plot to eradicate them through a string of "fortuitous" events.

Job shows God's grace in vindicating the sufferer's cry that his redeemer, who lives (19:25), will put all things right in this world or the next.

Psalms shows God's grace by reminding us of, and leading us in expressing, the *hesed* (relentless covenant love) God has for his people and the refuge that he is for them.

Proverbs shows us God's grace by opening up to us a world of wisdom in leading a life of happy godliness.

Ecclesiastes shows God's grace in its earthy reminder that the good things of life can never be pursued as the ultimate things of life and that it is God who in his mercy satisfies sinners (7:20; 8:11).

Song of Solomon shows God's grace and love for his bride by giving us a faint echo of it in the pleasures of faithful human sexuality.

Isaiah shows God's grace by reassuring us of his presence with and restoration of contrite sinners.

Jeremiah shows God's grace in promising a new and better covenant, one in which knowledge of God will be universally internalized.

Lamentations shows God's grace in his unfailing faithfulness in the midst of sadness.

Ezekiel shows God's grace in the divine heart surgery that cleansingly replaces stony hearts with fleshy ones.

Daniel shows God's grace in its repeated miraculous preservation of his servants.

Hosea shows God's grace in a real-live depiction of God's unstoppable love toward his whoring wife.

Joel shows God's grace in the promise to pour out his Spirit on all flesh.

Amos shows God's grace in the Lord's climactic promise of restoration in spite of rampant corruption.

Obadiah shows God's grace by promising judgment on Edom, Israel's oppressor, and restoration of Israel to the land in spite of current Babylonian captivity.

Jonah shows God's grace toward both immoral Nineveh and moral Jonah, irreligious pagans and a religious prophet, both of whom need and both of whom receive the grace of God.

Micah shows God's grace in the prophecy's repeated wonder at God's strange insistence on "pardoning iniquity and passing over transgression" (7:18).

Nahum shows God's grace in assuring Israel of "good news" and "peace," promising that the Assyrians have tormented them for the last time.

Habakkuk shows God's grace that requires nothing but trusting faith amid insurmountable opposition, freeing us to rejoice in God even in desolation.

Zephaniah shows God's grace in the Lord's exultant singing over his recalcitrant yet beloved people.

Haggai shows God's grace in promising a wayward people that the latter glory of God's (temple-ing) presence with them will far surpass its former glory.

Zechariah shows God's grace in the divine pledge to open up a fountain for God's people to "cleanse them from sin and uncleanness" (13:1).

Malachi shows God's grace by declaring the Lord's no-strings-attached love for his people.

Matthew shows God's grace in fulfilling the Old Testament promises of a coming king (5:17).

Mark shows God's grace as this coming king suffers the fate of a common criminal to buy back sinners (10:45).

Luke shows that God's grace extends to all the people one would not expect: hookers, the poor, tax collectors, sinners, and Gentiles. (19:10).

John shows God's grace in God's becoming one of us, flesh and blood (1:14), and dying and rising again so that by believing we might have life in his name (20:31).

Acts shows God's grace flooding out to all the world—starting in Jerusalem, ending in Rome; starting with Peter, apostle to the Jews, ending with Paul, apostle to the Gentiles (1:8).

Romans shows God's grace in Christ to the ungodly (4:5) while they were still sinners (5:8) that washes over both Jew and Gentile.

1 Corinthians shows God's grace in favoring what is lowly and foolish in the world (1:27).

2 Corinthians shows God's grace in channeling his power through weakness rather than strength (12:9).

Galatians shows God's grace in justifying both Jew and Gentile by Christ-directed faith rather than self-directed performance (2:16).

Ephesians shows God's grace in the divine resolution to unite us to his Son before time began (1:4).

Philippians shows God's grace in Christ's humiliating death on an instrument of torture—for us (2:8).

Colossians shows God's grace in nailing to the cross the record of debt that stood against us (2:14).

1 Thessalonians shows God's grace in providing the hope-igniting guarantee that Christ will return again (4:13).

2 Thessalonians shows God's grace in choosing us before time, that we might withstand Christ's greatest enemy (2:13).

1 Timothy shows God's grace in the radical mercy shown to "the chief of sinners" (1:15).

2 Timothy shows God's grace to be that which began (1:9) and that which fuels (2:1) the Christian life.

Titus shows God's grace in saving us by God's own cleansing mercy when we were most mired in sinful passions (3:5).

Philemon shows God's grace in transcending socially hierarchical structures with the deeper bond of Christ-won Christian brotherhood (v. 16).

Hebrews shows God's grace in giving his Son to be both our sacrifice to atone for us once and for all and our high priest to intercede for us forever (9:12).

James shows us God's grace by giving to those who have been born again "of his own will" (1:18) "wisdom from above" for meaningful godly living (3:17).

1 Peter shows God's grace in securing for us an unfading, imperishable inheritance, no matter what we suffer in this life (1:4).

2 Peter shows God's grace in guaranteeing the inevitability that one day all will be put right as the evil that has masqueraded as good will be unmasked at the coming Day of the Lord (3:10).

1 John shows God's grace in adopting us as his children (3:1).

2 and 3 John show God's grace in reminding specific individuals of "the truth that abides in us and will be with us forever" (2 John 2).

Jude shows God's grace in the Christ who presents us blameless before God in a world rife with moral chaos (v. 24).

Revelation shows God's grace in preserving his people through cataclysmic suffering, a preservation founded on the shed blood of the lamb (12:11).

Recommended Reading

Bridges, Jerry. *The Discipline of Grace: God's Role and Our Role in the Pursuit of Holiness.* Colorado Springs, CO: NavPress, 2006.

———. *Transforming Grace: Living Confidently in God's Unfailing Love.* Colorado Springs, CO: NavPress, 2008.

Brown, Steve. *A Scandalous Freedom: The Radical Nature of the Gospel.* West Monroe, LA: Howard, 2004.

———. *Three Free Sins: God's Not Mad at You.* New York: Howard Books, 2012.

Capon, Robert Farrar. *The Astonished Heart: Reclaiming the Good News from the Lost-and-Found of Church History.* Grand Rapids, MI: Eerdmans, 1996.

———. *Between Noon and Three: Romance, Law, and the Outrage of Grace.* Grand Rapids, MI: Eerdmans, 1997.

———. *Kingdom, Grace, Judgment: Paradox, Outrage, and Vindication in the Parables of Jesus.* Grand Rapids, MI: Eerdmans, 2002.

——— *The Romance of the Word: One Man's Love Affair with Theology.* Grand Rapids, MI: Eerdmans, 1995.

Chapell, Bryan. *Holiness by Grace: Delighting in the Joy That Is Our Strength.* Wheaton, IL: Crossway, 2001.

Elert, Werner. *Law and Gospel.* Philadelphia: Fortress Press, 1967.

Falsani, Cathleen. *Sin Boldly: A Field Guide for Grace.* Grand Rapids, MI: Zondervan, 2008.

Ferguson, Sinclair B. *By Grace Alone: How the Grace of God Amazes Me.* Lake Mary, FL: Reformation Trust, 2010.

———. *Grow in Grace.* Edinburgh: Banner of Truth, 1989.

Fitzpatrick, Elyse M. *Because He Loves Me: How Christ Transforms Our Daily Life.* Wheaton, IL: Crossway, 2010.

Fitzpatrick, Elyse M., and Jessica Thompson. *Give Them Grace: Dazzling Your Kids with the Love of Jesus.* Wheaton, IL: Crossway, 2011.

Forde, Gerhard O. *On Being a Theologian of the Cross: Reflections on Luther's Heidelberg Disputation, 1518.* Grand Rapids, MI: Eerdmans, 1997.

George, Timothy. *Amazing Grace: God's Pursuit, Our Response.* 2nd edition. Wheaton, IL: Crossway, 2011.

Giertz, Bo. *To Live with Christ: Devotions by Bo Giertz*. Translated by Richard Wood with Bror Erickson. St. Louis, MO: Concordia, 2008.

Hoekema, Anthony A. *Saved By Grace*. Grand Rapids, MI: Eerdmans, 1989.

Horton, Michael. *Putting Amazing Back into Grace: Embracing the Heart of the Gospel*. Revised and updated edition. Grand Rapids, MI: Baker, 2011.

Keller, Timothy. *The Prodigal God: Recovering the Heart of the Christian Faith*. New York: Riverhead, 2008.

Kleinig, John W. *Grace upon Grace: Spirituality for Today*. St. Louis, MO: Concordia, 2008.

Lloyd-Jones, Sally, and Jago. *Thoughts to Make Your Heart Sing*. Grand Rapids, MI: Zonderkidz, 2012.

Luther, Martin. *The Freedom of a Christian*. Translated by Mark D. Tranvik. Minneapolis: Fortress Press, 2008.

———. *Galatians*. Crossway Classic Commentaries. Edited by Alister McGrath and J. I. Packer. Wheaton, IL: Crossway, 1998.

Manning, Brennan. *Abba's Child: The Cry of the Heart for Intimate Belonging*. Expanded edition. Colorado Springs, CO: NavPress, 2002.

———. *All Is Grace: A Ragamuffin Memoir*. Colorado Springs, CO: David C. Cook, 2011.

———. *The Ragamuffin Gospel*. Sisters, OR: Multnomah, 2005.

May, Gerald G. *Addiction and Grace: Love and Spirituality in the Healing of Addictions*. New York: HarperOne, 1988.

Ortlund, Dane. *Defiant Grace: The Surprising Message and Mission of Jesus*. Carlisle, PA: EP Books, 2011.

Sproul, R. C. *What Is Reformed Theology? Understanding the Basics*. Grand Rapids, MI: Baker, 1997.

Swindoll, Charles R. *The Grace Awakening*. Nashville: Thomas Nelson, 2010.

Tchividjian, Tullian. *Jesus + Nothing = Everything*. Wheaton, IL: Crossway, 2011.

———. *Surprised by Grace: God's Relentless Pursuit of Rebels*. Wheaton, IL: Crossway, 2010.

Wilson, Jared C. *Gospel Deeps: Reveling in the Excellencies of Jesus*. Wheaton, IL: Crossway, 2012.

———. *Gospel Wakefulness*. Wheaton, IL: Crossway, 2011.

Yancey, Philip. *What's So Amazing about Grace?* Grand Rapids, MI: Zondervan, 1997.

Zahl, Paul F. M. *Grace in Practice: A Theology of Everyday Life*. Grand Rapids, MI: Eerdmans, 2007.

Notes

Chapter 1: Gratuitous and Undomesticated Grace

1. http://www.internetmonk.com/archive/grace-is-as-dangerous-as-ever.
2. Cathleen Falsani, *Sin Boldly: A Field Guide for Grace* (Grand Rapids, MI: Zondervan), 11.
3. J. Gresham Machen, *What Is Faith?* (Carlisle, PA: Banner of Truth, 1991), 173–74.
4. B. B. Warfield, *Selected Shorter Writings of Benjamin B. Warfield*, vol. 2, ed. John E. Meeter (Phillipsburg, NJ: Presbyterian & Reformed, 1970), 427.
5. John R. W. Stott, *Christ the Controversialist: A Study in Some Essentials of Evangelical Religion* (Downers Grove, IL: InterVarsity, 1970), 214.
6. Jerry Bridges, *Transforming Grace: Living Confidently in God's Unfailing Love* (Colorado Springs, CO: NavPress, 1993), 22.
7. Paul F. M. Zahl, *The Christianity Primer: Two Thousand Years of Amazing Grace* (Birmingham, AL: Palladium Press, 2005), 7.
8. Machen, *What Is Faith?*, 194.
9. This is a paraphrase of Paul F. M. Zahl's insight: "You have to be able to tell the difference between God's attacking voice of the law, his inhibiting and deposing voice, his voice that kills; and God's revivifying voice of grace, his creative and loving voice, his voice that makes alive." Paul F. M. Zahl, *Grace in Practice: A Theology of Everyday Life* (Grand Rapids, MI: Eerdmans, 2007), 66. See also Reinhold Niebuhr, "All . . . who live with any degree of serenity live by some assurance of grace." *The Essential Reinhold Niebuhr: Selected Essays and Addresses*, ed. Robert McAfee Brown (New Haven, CT: Yale University Press, 1987), 64.
10. Joel Green, "Grace," in T. Desmond Alexander and Brian S. Rosner, *New Dictionary of Biblical Theology* (Downers Grove, IL: InterVarsity, 2001), 524–27.

11. Michael Horton, *The Christian Faith: A Systematic Theology for Pilgrims On the Way* (Grand Rapids, MI: Zondervan, 2011), 267–68.
12. Karl Barth, *Church Dogmatics*, vol. 2, ed. G. W. Bromiley, T. F. Torrance, trans. T. H. L. Parker, W. B. Johnson, et al. (Edinburgh: T&T Clark, 1957), 356.
13. John Calvin, *Institutes of the Christian Religion*, ed. J. T. McNeil, trans. Ford Lewis Battles (Philadelphia: Westminster, 1960), 3.2.24.
14. Ibid., 3.31.7 and 2.17.1.
15. Ibid., 3.21.7 and 2.16.2.
16. Ibid., 2.7.4.
17. Ibid., 3.21.5 and 2.17.1.
18. Ibid.
19. "Grace proceeds entirely from within Himself, and that is conditioned in no way by anything in the objects of His favor." Burton Scott Easton, *The International Standard Bible Encyclopedia*, vol. 2, ed. James Orr (Grand Rapids, MI: Eerdmans, 1947), 1291. God "owes nothing to any counterpart. His grace condescension is free, i.e., unconditioned." Barth, *Church Dogmatics*, 355.
20. Robert Farrar Capon, *The Astonished Heart: Reclaiming the Good News from the Lost-and-Found of Church History* (Grand Rapids, MI: Eerdmans, 1996), 105.
21. Thomas F. Torrance, *God and Rationality* (London: Oxford University Press, 1971), 56.
22. Jacques Ellul, *Living Faith: Belief and Doubt in a Perilous World* (San Francisco: Harper & Row, 1983), 151–52.
23. James S. Stewart, *A Man in Christ*, quoted in James Fowler, "Grace of God," http://www.christinyou.net/pages/gracegod.html.
24. Alexander Schmemann, *For the Life of the World: Sacraments and Orthodoxy*, 2nd ed. (Crestwood, NY: St. Vladimir's Seminary Press, 1973), 19–20.
25. Robert F. Capon, *The Mystery of Christ . . . and Why We Don't Get It* (Grand Rapids, MI: Eerdmans, 1993), 62.
26. Machen, *What Is Faith?*, 174.
27. Green, "Grace," 524–27.
28. Ibid.
29. Ibid. In the Psalms, the singer frequently cries out in desperation or need, or thanks God for God's intervention. While this is a viable description of *hesed*, the underlying idea of God's covenant with his people is what makes the petition valid.
30. Ibid.
31. Ibid.

32. The "grace of God" is the merciful action of God in Christ by which people become believers. Believers are recipients of grace (Acts 11:23), are encouraged to continue in the grace of God (Acts 13:43; 20:32), and are to testify to the grace of God (Acts 20:24). "God's grace" also refers to the loving favor of God (Acts 14:3, 26; 15:40).
33. Twice the NT refers specifically to the grace of Jesus (Acts 15:11; 2 Pet. 3:18).
34. Ralph P. Martin and Peter H. Davids, *Dictionary of the Later New Testament and Its Developments* (Downers Grove, IL: InterVarsity, 2000), 58–62.
35. Green, "Grace," 524–27.
36. God's declaration about himself reappears frequently: Num. 14:17–19; Deut. 5:9–10; 7:9–13; Pss. 77:8–9; 86:5, 15; 103:8–12, 17–18; 111:4; 116:5; 145:8–9; Joel 2:12–14; Jon. 3:10–4:2; Neh. 9:17–19, 31–32; 2 Chron. 30:9. Much of this section is dependent on Green, "Grace," 524–27.
37. Green, "Grace."
38. Ibid.
39. Ibid.
40. Ibid.
41. Bo Giertz, *To Live with Christ: Devotions by Bo Giertz* (St. Louis, MO: Concordia, 2009), 24.
42. Werner Elert, *The Christian Ethos*, trans. Carl J. Schindler (Minneapolis: Muhlemberg Press, 1957), 187.
43. James Atkinson, *Martin Luther and the Birth of Protestantism* (London: Marshall, Morgan & Scott, 1982), 160.
44. Calvin, *Institutes* 2.7.8.
45. Quoted in Helmut Gollwitzer, *An Introduction to Protestant Theology*, trans. David Cairns (Louisville, KY: Westminster, 1982), 174.
46. "The reception of [the grace of God] is faith: faith means not doing something but receiving something; it means not the earning of a reward but the acceptance of a gift. A man can never be said to obtain a thing for himself if he obtains it by faith; indeed to say that he does not obtain it for himself but permits another to obtain it for him. Faith, in other words, is not active but passive; and to say that we are saved by faith is to say that we do not save ourselves but are saved only by the one in whom our faith is reposed; the faith of man presupposes the sovereign grace of God." Machen, *What Is Faith?*, 195.
47. Zahl, *Grace in Practice*, 64.
48. Hans Conzelmann, *Theological Dictionary of the New Testament*, vol. 9, ed. Gerhard Friedrich (Grand Rapids, MI: Eerdmans, 1974), 395.
49. *Shalom* is the Hebrew word for "peace."
50. This line is from the hymn "Joy to the World": "No more let sins and sorrows grow, / Nor thorns infest the ground; / He comes to make his blessings flow / Far as the curse is found, / Far as the curse is found, / Far as, far as the

curse is found." Isaac Watts, *Joy to the World!* (1719). The blessings of Jesus's redemption flow as far as the curse is found, wherever that curse is found. It is not a gospel simply for a disembodied existence on the other side of death. This hymn reminds us that the gospel is good news to a world where every aspect of the cosmos and our existence in it is twisted away from the intention of the Creator's design by the powers of sin and death.

51. James Fowler, "Grace of God."
52. H. H. Esser, "Charis," *New International Dictionary of New Testament Theology*, vol. 2, ed. C. Brown (Grand Rapids, MI: Zondervan, 1986), 119.
53. William Barclay, *The Mind of St. Paul* (New York: Collins, 1958), 127.
54. T. F. Torrance, *Theology in Reconstruction*, 183–90.
55. Martin Luther, *The Seven Penitential Psalms*, 1517, quoted in *Day by Day We Magnify Thee: Daily Readings* (Minneapolis: Fortress, 1982), 321.
56. Anne Lamott, *Traveling Mercies: Some Thoughts on Faith* (New York: Random House, 1999), 143.
57. In this book we will focus on what is called "efficacious grace." In systematic theology there are numerous ways to talk about grace: efficacious grace, common grace, and prevenient grace. Stanley Grenz, David Guretzki, and Cherith Fee Nordling offer concise descriptions of the options. "Efficacious grace" refers to the special application of grace to a person who comes by faith to Christ for salvation. This is also known as "redeeming grace." Common grace focuses on God's favor to all people and creation through providential care, regardless of whether they acknowledge and love God. "Prevenient grace" usually refers to the Wesleyan idea that God has enabled all people everywhere to respond favorably to the gospel if they so choose. Stanley Grenz, David Guretzki, and Cherith Fee Nordling, *Pocket Dictionary of Theological Terms* (Downers Grove, IL: InterVarsity, 1999), 56. For more on common grace, see Richard J, Mouw, *He Shines in All That's Fair: Culture and Common Grace* (Grand Rapids, MI: Eerdmans, 2002); and Abraham Kuyper, *Wisdom and Wonder: Common Grace in Science and Art*, ed. Jordan Ballor, Stephen Grabill, trans. Nelson Kloosterman (Grand Rapids, MI: Christian's Library Press, 2011). For insights from Reformed theologians on prevenient grace, see http://www.reformationfiles.com/files/displaytext.php?file=schreiner_prevenient.html; http://www.reformationtheology.com/2006/07/does_the_bible_teach_prevenien.php; and http://www.enjoyinggodministries.com/article/arminians-and-prevenient-grace/.

Chapter 2: Why We Need Grace

1. See the sevenfold use of "good": Gen. 1:4, 10, 12, 18, 21, 25, 31.
2. In the original language of Genesis this expression meant that God made humans "into" his image, much like one would say a potter makes a lump

of clay "into" a vase. That is to say, humanity is not *in* the image of God; we actually *are* the image of God.

3. Richard Pratt explains that "image of God" is a title of both humility and dignity. Humans are only finite, physical representations of their creator. We are images of God, but that is all that we are—images: "The Bible insists that we are not gods; we are merely *images* of God. We are not equal with our Maker; we don't have a spark of divinity within us. We are nothing more than creatures that reflect our Creator." Richard L. Pratt Jr., *Designed for Dignity: What God Has Made It Possible for You to Be* (Phillipsburg, NJ: P&R, 1993), 4. While this points to humility, "image of God" also reflects our dignity: "We are images, but we are images *of God* (Gen. 1:27). God did not make Adam and Eve to resemble rocks, trees, or animals. Nothing so common was in his design for us. Instead, God carefully shaped the first man and woman so that they were in *his* likeness. He determined to make us creatures of incomparable dignity" (Ibid., 8–9).
4. Francis Schaeffer writes: "So man has dominion over nature, but he uses it wrongly. The Christian is called upon to exhibit this dominion, but exhibit it rightly: treating the thing as having value itself, exercising dominion without being destructive. The church should always have taught and done this, but she has generally failed to do so, and we need to confess our failure. . . . By and large we must say that for a long, long time Christian teachers, including the best orthodox theologians, have shown a real poverty here." Francis Schaeffer and Udo Middlemann, *Pollution and the Death of Man* (Wheaton, IL: Tyndale, 1992), 72.
5. Pratt, *Designed For Dignity*, 22.
6. Ibid., 23.
7. Cornelius Plantinga Jr., *Not the Way It's Supposed to Be: A Breviary of Sin* (Grand Rapids, MI: Eerdmans, 1995), 10.
8. Isa. 32:14–20. Plantinga, *Not the Way It's Supposed to Be*, 10; Francis Brown, Samuel Rolles Driver, and Charles Augustus Briggs, *Enhanced Brown-Driver-Briggs Hebrew and English Lexicon*, electronic ed. (Oak Harbor, WA: Logos Research Systems, 2000), 1022.
9. Richard Pratt describes the effects of sin: "The rest of Scripture teaches that sin has affected every dimension of human character. We are totally depraved. To be sure, none of us are as bad as we could be. God restrains sin and enables us to avoid absolute ruin. When left to our own devices, however, we are utterly corrupted in all our faculties. Our thinking processes are so darkened that we twist and pervert the truth (1 Cor. 2:14; John 1:5; Rom. 8:7; Eph. 4:18; Titus 1:15). Our wills have been rendered unable to choose for spiritual good (John 8:34; 2 Tim. 3:2–4). Our affections have been marred and misdirected so that we love the world and its evil pleasures (John 5:42;

Heb. 3:12; 1 John 2:15–17). For these reasons, we are under the judgment of God (John 3:18–19) and are unable to do anything to redeem ourselves (John 6:44; 3:5; Rom. 7:18, 23). The sin of Adam and Eve has had devastating effects on human character." Pratt, *Designed for Dignity*, 51.

10. Paul David Tripp, *A Quest for More: Living for Something Bigger Than You* (Greensboro, NC: New Growth Press, 2008), 40.
11. Gen. 3:14–24. Plantinga writes: "The Bible presents sin by way of major concepts, principally lawlessness and faithlessness, expressed in an array of images: sin is the missing of a target, a wandering from the path, a straying from the fold. Sin is a hard heart and a stiff neck. Sin is blindness and deafness. It is both the overstepping of a line and the failure to reach it—both transgression and shortcoming. Sin is a beast crouching at the door. In sin, people attack or evade or neglect their divine calling. These and other images suggest deviance: even when it is familiar, sin is never normal. Sin is disruption of created harmony and then resistance to divine restoration of that harmony. Above all, sin disrupts and resists the vital human relation to God." Plantinga, *Not the Way It's Supposed to Be*, 5.
12. Ibid., 14.
13. Ibid., 30.
14. Ibid., 14.
15. Ibid., 13.
16. G. K. Beale, *We Become What We Worship: A Biblical Theology of Idolatry* (Downers Grove, IL: InterVarsity, 2008), 16.
17. Sigmund Freud serves unexpectedly as a theologian of original sin. In *A Short Account of Psychoanalysis* he writes that the "impulses . . . subjected to repression are those of selfishness and cruelty, which can be summed up in general as evil, but above all sexual wishful impulses, often of the crudest and most forbidden kind." Sigmund Freud, *A Short Account of Psychoanalysis*, Standard Edition 19, ed. and trans. James Strachey (London: Hogarth, 1953), 197. In *Civilization and Its Discontents* Freud writes: "Men are not gentle, friendly creatures wishing for love, who simply defend themselves if they are attacked, but that a powerful measure of desire for aggression has to be reckoned as part of their instinctual endowment. The result is that their neighbor is to them not only a possible helper or sexual object, but also a temptation to them to gratify their aggressiveness on him, to exploit his capacity for work without recompense, to use him sexually without his consent, to seize his possessions, to humiliate him, to cause him pain, to torture and kill him. *Homo homini lupus*; who has the courage to dispute it in the face of all the evidence in his own life and in history?" Sigmund Freud, *Civilization and Its Discontents*, trans. Joan Riviere (London: Hogarth, 1963), 58. Freud refers

to Thomas Hobbes's famous "Homo Homini Lupus Est," which is Latin for "man is a wolf to [his fellow] man.

18. D. G. Reid, "Violence," in *New Dictionary of Biblical Theology*, electronic ed., ed. T. Desmond Alexander and Brian S. Rosner (Downers Grove, IL: InterVarsity, 2001).
19. The word "curse" occurs five times in Genesis 4–11: 3:14, 17; 4:11; 5:29; 9:25.
20. Plantinga, *Not the Way It's Supposed to Be*, 16.
21. "Stories of Violence," in *Dictionary of Biblical Imagery*, ed. Leland Ryken, JimWilhoit, and Tremper Longman III (Downers Grove, IL: InterVarsity, 1998), 916.
22. Plantinga, *Not the Way It's Supposed to Be*, 197.
23. Ibid., 16.
24. Dan B. Allender, "The Mark of Evil," in *God and the Victim: Theological Reflections on Evil, Victimization, Justice, and Forgiveness*, ed. Lisa Barnes Lampman (Grand Rapids, MI: Eerdmans, 1999), 52.

Chapter 3: God's Redeeming Grace in the Old Testament

1. Andrew J. Schmutzer, "A Theology of Sexual Abuse: A Reflection on Creation and Devastation," *Journal of the Evangelical Theological Society* 51 (2008): 802n98.
2. While this could be the first sacrifice, it is not *necessarily* the first sacrifice. It can be characterized as "theological allusion" where Adam and Eve did not understand what God did as atoning sacrifice, but later generations of readers have come to see the symbolism.
3. E. J. Young, *Genesis 3* (Edinburgh: Banner of Truth, 1966), 149.
4. In the Bible, nakedness often represents unrighteousness. It symbolizes the ideas of judgment and humiliation in the biblical world. The Bible pictures the sinner as clothed in "filthy rags" or "naked and ashamed." The prophets described the sinful state of the nation of Israel as "nakedness" before God and the world (Isa. 47:3; Lam. 1:8; Ezek. 16:36). "'Remove the filthy garments from him.' And to him he said, 'Behold, I have taken your iniquity away from you, and I will clothe you with pure vestments'" (Zech. 3:4). "I will greatly rejoice in the Lord; my soul shall exult in my God, for he has clothed me with the garments of salvation; he has covered me with the robe of righteousness" (Isa. 61:10). Adam and Eve were ashamed because of their unrighteousness. They were not able to stand naked in God's holy and righteous presence. Their consciences were deformed, their joy was turned to shame, and their relationship with God was corrupted. This happened because sin stripped them of the right standing with which they were created. By his grace, God created them in right standing. God responded to

their calamity with an immediate act of mercy. He covered their shame. With animal skins God made temporary coverings of "righteousness" for them: "Unto Adam also and to his wife did the Lord God make coats of skins, and clothed them" (Gen. 3:21 KJV). God did not accept the fig leaves. He would only accept a cover that he alone had put on them. R. C. Sproul writes, "It may be said that the first act of God's redemptive grace occurred when he condescended to clothe his embarrassed fallen creatures." R. C. Sproul, *Faith Alone: The Evangelical Doctrine of Justification* (Grand Rapids, MI: Baker, 1999), 102. God in grace clothed these unrighteous first sinners with the skins of a sacrifice, made with his own hands, so that they could come to him and be saved.

5. Cornelius Plantinga Jr., *Not the Way It's Supposed to Be: A Breviary of Sin* (Grand Rapids, MI: Eerdmans, 1995), 199.
6. "Whole," in *Dictionary of Biblical Imagery*, ed. Leland Ryken, Jim Wilhoit, and Tremper Longman III (Downers Grove, IL: InterVarsity, 1998), 944.
7. Stephen G. Dempster, *Dominion and Dynasty: A Theology of the Hebrew Bible*, New Studies in Biblical Theology 15 (Downers Grove, IL: InterVarsity, 2003), 72.
8. Paul R. Williamson, *Sealed with an Oath: Covenant in God's Unfolding Purpose*, New Studies in Biblical Theology 23 (Downers Grove, IL: InterVarsity, 2007), 60–61.
9. Ibid., 76.
10. Mark Driscoll and Gerry Breshears, *Doctrine: What Christians Should Believe* (Wheaton, IL: Crossway, 2010), 180.
11. *Hesed* is the OT word for God's compassionate love. It is used 254 times. The NT word is *charis* (charity), and it is used over 150 times. *Hesed* refers to compassionate acts performed either spontaneously or in response to an appeal by one in dire straits. *Hesed* is not grounded in obligation or contract. The acts arise out of affection and goodness. *Charis* is about favor and friendship as well as gifts from benefactors. Acts of *hesed* pertain to covenantal relations, but God enters into covenant with human beings freely; the establishment of the covenant is itself an act of *hesed* on God's part. *Charis* connotes spontaneous kindness and acts of generosity grounded in dispositions of compassion toward those in need.
12. Stephen G. Dempster, "Exodus and Biblical Theology: On Moving into the Neighborhood with a New Name," *Southern Baptist Journal of Theology* 12/3 (2008): 4. The importance of the exodus in the theology of the Hebrew Bible is breathtaking: "There are over 120 explicit OT references to the Exodus in law, narrative, prophecy and psalm, and it is difficult to exaggerate its importance. Foundational to Israel's self-perception (Deut. 6:20–25)—they are here first designated a people (Exod. 1:9)—it is recalled in liturgy (e.g. Ps.

78, 105; Exod. 12:26–27), prayer (e.g. 2 Sam. 7:23; Jer. 32:16–21; Dan 9:4–19), and sermon (e.g. Josh. 24; Judg. 2:11–13; 1 Sam. 12:6–8; 1 Kings 8). As the pre-eminent saving event in their history (Deut. 4:32–40), the Exodus profoundly shaped Israel's social structures, calendars, remembrance of the ancient past, and hopes of future restoration." Rikki E. Watts, "Exodus," in *New Dictionary of Biblical Theology*, ed. T. Desmond Alexander and Brian S. Rosner (Downers Grove, IL: InterVarsity, 2001), 478–87.

13. Dempster, "Exodus and Biblical Theology," 4–5.
14. Peter Enns, "Exodus, Book of," in *New Dictionary of Biblical Theology*.
15. Dempster, "Exodus and Biblical Theology," 9.
16. D. G. Reid, "Violence," in *New Dictionary of Biblical Theology*, electronic ed., ed. T. Desmond Alexander and Brian S. Rosner (Downers Grove, IL: InterVarsity, 2001).
17. Christopher J. H. Wright, *The Mission of God: Unlocking the Bible's Grand Narrative* (Downers Grove, IL: InterVarsity, 2006), 272.
18. John Goldingay, *Old Testament Theology*, vol. 1: *Israel's Gospel* (Downers Grove, IL: InterVarsity, 2003), 302.
19. Wright, *The Mission of God*, 271.
20. The Passover is a sacrifice (Ex. 12:27; 34:25). It is described as "the LORD's offering" (Num. 9:7, 13), and the verb "to sacrifice" is used in reference to it (Deut. 16:2, 4, 5, 6).
21. Dempster, *Dominion and Dynasty*, 99.
22. Leon Morris, *The Atonement: Its Meaning and Significance* (Downers Grove, IL: InterVarsity, 1983), 89.
23. Steve Jeffery, Michael Ovey, and Andrew Sach, *Pierced for Our Transgressions: Rediscovering the Glory of Penal Substitution* (Wheaton, IL: Crossway, 2007), 34.
24. Dempster, "Exodus and Biblical Theology," 12.
25. See Lev. 10:1; Morris, *The Atonement*, 68.
26. Jeffery, Ovey, and Sach, *Pierced for Our Transgressions*, 42.
27. D. A. Carson, R. T. France, and J. A. Motyer, *New Bible Commentary: 21st Century Edition*, ed. Gordon J. Wenham (Downers Grove, IL: IVP Academic, 1994).
28. David Peterson, "Atonement in The Old Testament," in *Where Wrath and Mercy Meet: Proclaiming the Atonement Today* (Carlisle, UK: Paternoster, 2001), 11.
29. Jeffery, Ovey, and Sach, *Pierced for Our Transgressions*, 49.
30. Stanley Grenz, David Guretzki, and Cherith Fee Nordling, *Pocket Dictionary of Theological Terms* (Downers Grove, IL: InterVarsity, 1999), 96.
31. Ibid., 50.
32. "Atonement," in *Dictionary of Biblical Imagery*, 55.

33. Williamson, *Sealed with an Oath*, 111.
34. According to Dumbrell, in the Aramaic translation of Isaiah 53 "the Servant is defined as the messiah." William J. Dumbrell, *Search for Order: Biblical Eschatology in Focus* (Eugene, OR: Wipf & Stock, 2001), 120.
35. Jeffery, Ovey, and Sach, *Pierced for Our Transgressions*, 54.
36. Graham A. Cole, *God the Peacemaker: How Atonement Brings Shalom*, New Studies in Biblical Theology 25 (Downers Grove, IL: InterVarsity, 2009), 100–101.
37. Reid, "Violence," 834.
38. Jeffery, Ovey, and Sach, *Pierced for Our Transgressions*, 57.
39. Alan J. Groves, "Atonement in Isaiah 53," in *The Glory of the Atonement: Biblical, Theological, and Practical Perspectives*, ed. C. E. Hill and F. A. James III (Downers Grove, IL: InterVarsity, 2004), 81.
40. Jeffery, Ovey, and Sach, *Pierced for Our Transgressions*, 61.
41. Plantinga, *Not the Way It's Supposed to Be*, 9–10.
42. Isa. 9:6–7. Other similar passages include Mic. 5:2–5 and Eph. 2:14. While some scholars would disagree, I would also include Ps. 72:7 in this list of passages. It, too, connects the reign of the future messianic king with the coming of *shalom*: "In his days may the righteous flourish, and peace (Heb. *shalom*) abound, till the moon be no more!" John H. Sailhamer, *The Meaning of the Pentateuch: Revelation, Composition, and Interpretation* (Downers Grove, IL: InterVarsity, 2009), 499–503.
43. See "Index of Allusions and Verbal Parallels," in *The Greek New Testament*, 4th ed., ed. B. Aland et al. (Stuttgart, Germany: Deutsche Biblegesellschaft, 2001), 891–901.
44. "Stories of Violence," in *Dictionary of Biblical Imagery*, 916.

Chapter 4: God's Redeeming Grace in the New Testament

1. D. G. Reid, "Violence," in *New Dictionary of Biblical Theology*, ed. T. Desmond Alexander and Brian S. Rosner, electronic ed. (Downers Grove, IL: InterVarsity, 2001), 832.
2. Ibid., 834.
3. 1 Cor. 15:1–4: "Now I would remind you, brothers, of the gospel I preached to you, which you received, in which you stand, and by which you are being saved, if you hold fast to the word I preached to you—unless you believed in vain. For I delivered to you as of first importance what I also received: that Christ died for our sins in accordance with the Scriptures, that he was buried, that he was raised on the third day in accordance with the Scriptures."
4. The four Gospels (Matthew, Mark, Luke, and John) were written to "bring together the words and deeds of the historical Jesus in a way that demon-

strates the significance of his life, death, and resurrection." John H. Sailhamer, *The Life of Christ* (Grand Rapids, MI: Zondervan, 1995), 10.

5. Tim Keller, "Redeemer Core Values," http://www.redeemer.com/about_us/vision_and_values/core_values.html.
6. Tim Keller, "The Gospel in All Its Forms," *Leadership Journal* (Spring 2008): 75.
7. Augustine, "Sermon CLXXXV: Christmas #2," in *Sermons to the People: Advent, Christmas, New Year's, Epiphany*, ed. and trans. William Griffin (New York: Doubleday, 2002), 65.
8. "The Fourth Gospel's primary focus is the mission of Jesus: He is the one who comes into the world, accomplishes his work and returns to the Father; he is the one who descended from heaven and ascends again; he is the Sent One, who, in complete dependence and perfect obedience to his sender, fulfills the purpose for which the Father sent him." Andreas J. Köstenberger and Peter T. O'Brien, *Salvation to the Ends of the Earth: A Biblical Theology of Mission* (Downers Grove, IL: InterVarsity, 2001), 203.
9. There are seven so-called "I Am" sayings in John's Gospel. Jesus is: the bread of life (6:35, 48, 51); the light of the world (8:12; 9:5); the gate (10:7, 9); the good shepherd (10:11, 14); the resurrection and the life (11:25); the way and the truth and the life (14:6); and the true vine (15:1).
10. Rev. Samuel Billy Kyles, interviewed by Liane Hansen, *Weekend Edition Sunday*, NPR, January 17, 2010, http//www.npr.org/templates/story/story.php?StoryId-122670935.
11. David Powlison, "God's Grace in Your Sufferings," in *Suffering and the Sovereignty of God*, ed. John Piper and Justin Taylor (Wheaton, IL: Crossway, 2006), 172.
12. Matthew describes Jesus as the one who was born of a virgin and who was conceived by the third person of the Trinity, the omnipotent Holy Spirit (Matt. 1:20). At his baptism, we read that Jesus is God's beloved Son, in whom God is well pleased (3:17). Jesus is the one on whom the Holy Spirit descended like a dove (3:16). Jesus is the one who defeated Satan in the desert and who afterward was ministered to by myriads of angels (4:1–11). Jesus is the one who cleansed lepers, gave sight to the blind, healed the deaf, and cast out demons by simply speaking (8:1–4; 9:27–31; 8:28–34). Jesus is the one who taught the Scriptures with authority and who fulfilled prophecies (7:28–29). Jesus is the one whose wisdom was far greater than that of Solomon (12:42). Jesus is the one who said, "Heaven and earth will pass away, but my words will not pass away" (24:35). Jesus is the one who fed over five thousand people with five loaves and two fish (14:13–21). Jesus is the one who was transfigured in such a way that his face shone like the brightness of the noonday sun (17:1–13). Jesus is the one who predicted his death and res-

urrection in detail before they actually happened (17:22–23). Jesus is the one who is King of the Jews and who rode into Jerusalem on a donkey (21:1–11). Jesus is the one who pleaded with his Father in the garden of Gethsemane, saying: "Let this cup pass from me. . . . Not as I will, but as you will" (26:39). Jesus is the one who kept silent before his accusers (27:14). Jesus is the one who was betrayed, forsaken, arrested, mocked, beaten, slapped, flogged, spat upon, stripped naked, crowned with thorns, and crucified on a cross outside Jerusalem (26–27). Jesus is the one who purchased the new covenant with his blood, which was poured out for the forgiveness of sins (26:28). Jesus is the one who fully drank the cup of God's wrath (27:45–54). Jesus is the one who died, who was buried, and who rose again on the third day (27:45–28:10). Jesus is the one who was given all authority in heaven and on earth (28:18). Jesus is the one who appeared to his disciples and commanded them to make disciples of all nations (28:19–20).

13. Sailhamer, *The Life of Christ*, 22.
14. Mark Driscoll and Gerry Breshears, *Death by Love: Letters from the Cross* (Wheaton, IL: Crossway, 2008), 17.
15. R. W. Yarbrough, "Atonement," in *New Dictionary of Biblical Theology*, 388.
16. For an extended exegetical, theological, and historical defense of penal substitutionary atonement see Steve Jeffery, Michael Ovey, and Andrew Sach, *Pierced for Our Transgressions: Rediscovering the Glory of Penal Substitution* (Wheaton, IL: Crossway, 2007).
17. Ibid., 23.
18. Ibid., 67.
19. For a fuller exposition of this idea see Graham A. Cole, *God the Peacemaker: How Atonement Brings Shalom*, New Studies in Biblical Theology 25 (Downers Grove, IL: InterVarsity, 2009), 169–73.
20. Luke 9:31. "Jesus goes down to 'Egypt' and suffers oppression, completely submitting to the penalty of sin and death and, thus, paving the way for the Exodus of all peoples into the glorious liberty of the children of God! This firstborn son's blood is not spared but becomes the blood of the covenant sprinkled on the nations not as self-curse, but as a balm of cleansing, renewal, and forgiveness, binding them to him forever." Stephen G. Dempster, "Exodus and Biblical Theology: On Moving into the Neighborhood with a New Name," *Southern Baptist Journal of Theology* 12/3 (2008): 19–20.
21. "In the developing New Testament, Exodus language is pervasive. Herod's brutal murder of the infants in the district of Bethlehem echoes the slaughter of the Israelite newborns in Egypt (Matt. 2:16–18). Jesus' descent into Egypt and exodus from it as a child mirrors early Israel's experience (Matt. 2:13–15). His depiction as a new Moses giving his new commandments from the Mount is in both continuity and contrast with the old Moses at

Sinai (Matthew 5–7). His feeding of the crowds in the wilderness with bread shows that he is the ultimate manna come down from heaven (John 6:35). His last supper recalls the original Passover, and his words of institution regarding the blood of the covenant deliberately recall Moses' words to the Israelites when sealing the Sinai covenant (Matt. 26:28, cf. Ex. 24:8). His entire life and ministry is viewed as the antitype of the tabernacle built at Sinai: The Word became flesh and moved into the neighborhood and we beheld his glory—not the old glory of the cloud filling the tent—but 'the glory of the One and Only, who came from the Father, full of grace and truth' (John 1:14 NIV; cf. Ex. 34:5). Those who dwell in the midst of this tabernacle, leave with a face set on fire by the divine presence, just like Moses (2 Cor. 3; cf. Ex. 34:29–35)." Dempster, "Exodus and Biblical Theology," 5–6.

22. John Murray, *Redemption Accomplished and Applied* (Grand Rapids, MI: Eerdmans, 1984), 42–43.
23. N. T. Wright, *Following Jesus: Biblical Reflections on Discipleship* (Grand Rapids, MI: Eerdmans, 1994), 17. See also N. T. Wright, *Colossians and Philemon*, Tyndale New Testament Commentaries (Downers Grove, IL: InterVarsity, 1986), 60–63.
24. 1 Pet. 1:18–19. Regarding forgiveness, J, Gresham Machen writes: "There may be some foul spot in our lives; the kind of thing that the world never forgives, the kind of thing, at any rate, for which we who know all can never forgive ourselves. But what care we whether the world forgives, if God has received us by the death of His Son?" J. Gresham, Machen, *What Is Faith?* (Carlisle, PA: Banner of Truth, 1991), 82.
25. Jerry Bridges, *The Gospel for Real Life: Turn to the Liberating Power of the Cross . . . Every Day* (Colorado Springs: Navpress, 2002), 74.
26. J. I. Packer and Mark Dever, *In My Place Condemned He Stood: Celebrating the Glory of the Atonement* (Wheaton, IL: Crossway, 2007), 47.
27. Ibid.
28. Bridges, *The Gospel for Real Life*, 75.
29. Paul F. M. Zahl, *Grace in Practice: A Theology of Everyday Life* (Grand Rapids, MI: Eerdmans, 2007), 118.
30. Jeffery, Ovey, and Sach, *Pierced for Our Transgressions*, 151–2.
31. Packer and Dever, *In My Place Condemned He Stood*, 35.
32. John Murray, *The Atonement* (Philadelphia: P&R, 1962), 15.
33. Charles Spurgeon, "'Love and I'—A Mystery," sermon, Metropolitan Tabernacle, Newington, UK (July 2, 1882), http://www.ccel-org/ccel/spurgeon/sermons28. titlepage.html.
34. Francis Turretin, *Institutes of Elenctic Theology* (Phillipsburg, NJ: P&R, 1993), 2:447.

35. John Calvin, *Institutes of the Christian Religion*, ed. J. T. McNeil, trans. Ford Lewis Battles (Philadelphia: Westminster, 1960), 3.9.3.
36. Quoted in Charles Hodge, *Systematic Theology* (Edinburgh: Hendrickson, 1999), 3:148.
37. Martin Luther, *Werke* (Weimar, 1883), 5:608.
38. Mark Driscoll, *Doctrine: What Christians Should Believe* (Wheaton: Crossway, 2010), 303.
39. Robert Sherman, *King, Priest, and Prophet: A Trinitarian Theology of Atonement* (New York: T&T Clark, 2004), 166.
40. "A leading ingredient in the Bible's eschatological images of the future age is the restored wholeness that glorified saints will finally enjoy in perpetuity. The book of Revelation contains all the important biblical motifs (which can be found scattered through OT apocalyptic visions as well). One is the union of people with God and Christ, pictured as a marriage (Rev. 19:7; 21:2, 9) and as an existence in which the redeemed 'follow the Lamb wherever he goes' (Rev. 14:4 RSV). To be whole is to be one with the God whose 'dwelling . . . is among mortals' (Rev. 21:3 NRSV). Social wholeness is also present, imaged in the single city where all the redeemed will reside through all eternity (cf. Jesus' homey image of heaven as a stately house with many rooms [Jn 14:2]). Inner wholeness is marked by the true shalom of God, which replaces pain and tears with healing and compassion (Rev 21:4). Feelings of insecurity and alienation will be replaced with security and intimacy (Rev. 21:3). Here is the ultimate fulfillment of Isaiah's prophecy regarding the suffering servant, that 'upon him was the chastisement that made us whole' (Is. 53:5 RSV)." "Whole," in *Dictionary of Biblical Imagery*, ed. Leland Ryken, Jim Wilhoit, and Tremper Longman III (Downers Grove, IL: InterVarsity, 1998), 944.
41. R. W. Yarbrough, "Atonement," in *New Dictionary of Biblical Theology*. A redeemed people from every tribe, nation, and tongue will dwell in the heavenly city because their names are written in the Lamb's book of life (Rev. 21:27). Only blood-bought sinners saved by the Lamb will dwell in the heavenly city (Rev. 5:9–10). The heavenly city will display a beautiful mosaic of redemption. Peoples from every tribe and tongue will bring their honor and glory into the city and offer praise to God and to the Lamb (Rev. 21:24–26).
42. Christopher J. H. Wright, *The Mission of God: Unlocking the Bible's Grand Narrative* (Downers Grove, IL: IVP Academic, 2006), 529–30.
43. D. A. Carson, *A Call to Spiritual Reformation: Priorities from Paul and His Prayers* (Grand Rapids, MI: Baker, 1992), 189.
44. The Heidelberg Catechism, Question and Answer 1. http://www.ccel.org/creeds/heidelberg-cat.html.

Chapter 5: It's Grace All the Way

1. Augustine, *Against the Two Letters of the Pelagians*, I.iii.6.
2. John Calvin, *Institutes of the Christian Religion*, ed. J. T. McNeil, trans. Ford Lewis Battles (Philadelphia: Westminster, 1960), 2.3.14.
3. John Bunyan, *Grace Abounding to the Chief of Sinners*, para. 228–32.
4. The Cambridge Declaration describes being saved by grace alone: "We reaffirm that in salvation we are rescued from God's wrath by his grace alone. It is the supernatural work of the Holy Spirit that brings us to Christ by releasing us from our bondage to sin and raising us from spiritual death to spiritual life. We deny that salvation is in any sense a human work. Human methods, techniques or strategies by themselves cannot accomplish this transformation. Faith is not produced by our unregenerated human nature." http://www.reformed.org/documents/cambridge.html.
5. The Cambridge Declaration describes being saved by faith alone: "We reaffirm that justification is by grace alone through faith alone because of Christ alone. In justification Christ's righteousness is imputed to us as the only possible satisfaction of God's perfect justice. We deny that justification rests on any merit to be found in us, or upon the grounds of an infusion of Christ's righteousness in us, or that an institution claiming to be a church that denies or condemns sola fide can be recognized as a legitimate church." http://www.reformed.org/documents/cambridge.html.
6. Peter T. O'Brien, *The Letter to the Ephesians*, Pillar New Testament Commentary (Grand Rapids, MI: Eerdmans, 1999), 178.
7. Tet-Lim N. Yee, *Jews, Gentiles and Ethnic Reconciliation: Paul's Jewish Identity and Ephesians*, Society for New Testament Studies Monograph Series 130 (Cambridge: Cambridge University Press, 2005), 64.
8. One commentator calls it "the most effective summary we have of the Pauline doctrine of salvation by grace through faith." C. L. Mitton, cited in Klyne Snodgrass, *Ephesians*, NIV Application Commentary (Grand Rapids, MI: Zondervan, 1996), 94.
9. There has been some debate as to what the word "this" refers to in the phrase "this is not your own doing" (2:8), whether "faith" or "grace." But probably the answer is neither, since the pronoun "this" in Greek is in the neuter gender, and "faith" and "grace" are both feminine. It is best to see "this" as referring to the whole process of salvation, not one particular aspect (though, of course, both grace and faith are included in salvation). See Frank Thielman, *Ephesians*, Baker Exegetical Commentary on the New Testament (Grand Rapids, MI: Baker Academic, 2010), 143n2.
10. Andrew T. Lincoln, *Ephesians*, Word Biblical Commentary (Dallas: Word, 1990), 116.
11. Snodgrass, *Ephesians*, 106.

12. These are taken from Thielman, *Ephesians*, 144.
13. On this point see also Lincoln, *Ephesians*, 113: "Since salvation is seen as a creation in Christ for good works, such works cannot be the cause of their salvation."
14. O'Brien, *Ephesians*, 178; emphasis original.
15. Dietrich Bonhoeffer, *The Cost of Discipleship* (New York: Touchstone, 1995), 45.
16. Steve Brown, A *Scandalous Freedom: The Radical Nature of the Gospel* (West Monroe, LA: Howard, 2004), 12–13.
17. For this section I am indebted to James Fowler, "Grace of God," http://www.christinyou.net/pages/gracegod.html.
18. For the phrase "end of the earth" see Isa. 49:6; Acts 1:8; 13:47. Also notice "all nations" in Matt. 28:19.

Concluding Prayer

1. *The Valley of Vision: A Collection of Puritan Prayers and Devotions*, ed. Arthur Bennett (Edinburgh: Banner of Truth, 1975), 284–85.

Appendix

1. Adapted from Dane Ortlund, "The Grace of God in the Bible," http://dogmadoxa.blogspot.com/2010/09/grace-of-god-in-bible.html. Used by permission.

RE:LIT

Resurgence Literature (Re:Lit) is a ministry of the Resurgence. At theResurgence.com you will find free theological resources in blog, audio, video, and print forms, along with information on forthcoming conferences, to help Christians contend for and contextualize Jesus's gospel. At ReLit.org you will also find the full lineup of Resurgence books for sale. The elders of Mars Hill Church have generously agreed to support Resurgence and the Acts 29 Church Planting Network in an effort to serve the entire church.

FOR MORE RESOURCES

Re:Lit – relit.org
Resurgence – theResurgence.com
Re:Train – retrain.org
Mars Hill Church – marshill.org
Acts 29 – acts29network.org